INTEGRATING TEENAGERS INTO ... RCH

# ONE BODY

## SAM HALVERSON

Our churches have become silos, and in this thought-provoking yet practical book, Sam Halverson calls us to do something about it. *One Body* is a necessary read for all who believe that people and relationships are more important than programs.

**Chanon Ross, Ph.D.**
**Director, Institute for Youth Ministry**
**Princeton Theological Seminary**

It's now almost universally agreed in the world of youth ministry that we've got to stop isolating our teenagers from the rest of the church. Isolation hurts teenagers and hamstrings the church. But up to this point, we've had few prototypes for making that seismic shift. With *One Body*, Sam helps us imagine a church without generational isolation and makes a compelling, practical case that integrating teenagers into our congregations really can happen. I can't think of a single church that won't benefit from this book.

**Mark DeVries is the author of *Family-Based Youth Ministry*, the founder of Ministry Architects, and served 28 years as a youth pastor in Nashville, Tennessee.**

Sam Halverson offers biblically grounded, theologically rich arguments for why churches must move away from the silo model of ministry that perpetuates the isolation and alienation of youth from the church, while providing compelling examples and ideas to show us how this can be done. Anyone committed to building a church alive with the energy and prophetic insight of young people should read this…and then show it to every leader in their congregation.

**Dr. Elizabeth Corrie, Assistant Professor in the Practice of Youth Education and Peacebuilding and Director of the Youth Theological Initiative at Candler School of Theology, Emory University**

# One Body

Publisher: Mark Oestreicher
Managing Editor: Laura Gross
Editor: Tara Van Dyke
Cover Design: Adam McLane
Layout: Adam McLane
Creative Director: Matt Foley

THE HOLY BIBLE, NEW INTERNATIONAL VERSION®, NIV® Copyright © 1973, 1978, 1984, 2011 by Biblica, Inc.® Used by permission. All rights reserved worldwide.

ISBN-13: 978-0-9910050-8-6
ISBN-10: 0991005082

The Youth Cartel, LLC
www.theyouthcartel.com
Email: info@theyouthcartel.com

Born in San Diego
Printed in the U.S.A.

To all of the faith communities of the North Georgia United Methodist Conference (not just the ones with youth programming). You are called to be the presence of Christ to the young. Encounter the kingdom together.

# CONTENTS

# ACKNOWLEDGMENTS

Thanks to my youth ministry tribe from the 2011 Nashville Youth Ministry Coaching Program—Shawn Kiger, Emily Capes, Daniel Longden, Mike Pitts, Kordell Sims, Greg Turner, Cindy Vestal, Jonathan Odom, Kevin Libick, and our coach, Mark Oestreicher. Your insight and support continue to guide and encourage me in my youth ministry. The Youth Cartel's YMCP is the single most effective training and support I've encountered for my current understanding of the importance of youth integration into the church.

I am also grateful to the older adults in the churches where I've served. You welcomed a younger minister into your fold and accepted the youth to whom we were all called to minister. Your willingness to build relationships with the youth—especially when you weren't volunteers in the youth program—continues to make an impact on the lives you touched.

Thanks also to the senior pastors with whom I've served. You encouraged me to move beyond the youth room and into the lives of the "rest of the congregation." Integrating the minister into the whole community is the first step of bringing the youth out of the silo.

# INTRODUCTION

I like to go to parties.

In over 30 years of youth ministry, I've been invited to many graduation parties. Though each uniquely celebrates a particular student, they are basically very similar events: friends and family, lots of food, pictures, hanging out, and remembering things past.

So I expected the same when I attended Emma's graduation party.

Emma's house had a pool, a big yard, and a lake out back. Loud music played, and welcoming calls came from youth and families on the deck. After greeting Emma, thanking her mom for the invitation, and making a few introductions, I made my way to the food.

That's where I started noticing this party was unique.

As I walked from the food table to the deck, by the pool, across the yard, and towards the lake, I encountered groups of people that had nothing to do with the others at the party. I began to notice a sharp separation between the groups of partygoers.

The living room was Xbox central. Emma's cousins from out of town were fully absorbed in their video gaming and paid little attention to anyone else. On the deck were Emma's church friends—the crowd I knew and felt comfortable with.

The expansive yard had room for multiple games. College students—friends of Emma's older sister—played volleyball on the lawn and seemed fairly welcoming to anyone who came near their game. Emma's younger brother shot hoops in the

driveway with neighborhood friends. Every now and then, kids ran to the food table to fill a plate with chicken wings, sausages, or sliders and then rejoined their games in progress. A few huge camper RVs occupied the other side of the driveway. Some of Emma's relatives sat inside one of the vehicles playing cards, talking, and enjoying whatever food they had gathered from the party to take back to their RV home base.

But the tent village set up between the woods and the lake really caught my eye. About five tents showed evidence of people settled in for a few days. Wet towels and bathing suits hung from laundry lines strung between trees. Three motorcycles were parked nearby. Another vehicle stood with doors open and classic rock playing from its speakers—the music sometimes in discord with the Top 40 tunes playing by the pool. A campfire burned in the midst of it all, and dirty pans sat on a makeshift grill. The tent residents were lined up along the shore of the lake (one in a canoe not far offshore), and they were fishing. That's right. They were fishing. With a beer in one hand and a pole in the other, these guys were quite a contrast from the church members sipping lemonade by the pool. Emma's dad told me the campers were his buddies from work. They had been there for two days already and were probably staying another day, or until the beer ran out.

The diversity of the crowd made this party quite unique. Bikers, campers, teens, kids, grandparents, ministers, family, friends—divided into groups, but all there to celebrate Emma's graduation. As I stood at the food table later on—munching on shrimp and dipping green pepper slices into the veggie dip—I realized the table was the one place where this vast mixture of people converged. Every now and then, people would venture from a camper to fill a plate or a glass. Some walked in from poolside to refill a bowl of chips. There seemed to be a steady stream from the lake going back and forth to the cooler, grabbing another drink and placing a burger on a plate. Even the video-gaming kids walked in from time to time to find more sustenance.

Seldom did any of these people make conversation with anyone else from the different groups. They would walk in, get some food, maybe say hello to the host, and then walk back out to their own sacred space. Since I'd planted myself by the food table, Emma's mom had introduced me to most of the people who stopped by.

When I reflect back on Emma's party, I realize my vantage point allowed me to enjoy the company of more people than almost anyone else there at the party. Most guests drifted to and from the table, quickly moving back to their own comfortable space. But at the table, I heard stories about Emma from every different group at that party. Stories and reflections from cousins, church families, teachers, and friends gave me a greater appreciation and understanding of Emma—her life, her motivations, her dreams, and the things that helped form her. Through interaction with the diverse group of guests, I participated deeply in the celebration and received the blessing of knowing Emma better than ever.

Perhaps you can connect with some of my experiences from that day.

If we step back from the story and allow it to move into other areas of our lives, we might find some similar experiences at the "table" and in the "safe places" of our churches—sanctuaries and youth rooms or fellowship halls and youth ministry wings. When teenagers spend time away from the rest of the church, we miss some of the most important blessings of what it means to be a community of faith bound together by the gospel. We allow our youth (and our children—but that's a book for someone else to write) to take refuge in programs and

buildings specifically designed for them, convincing ourselves that teenagers want these "tribal places" where they can spend time with their own kind.

The problem is that human beings—and especially teenagers—don't always want what's best, and sometimes people say they want one thing when what they really want is something else. Sometimes we choose to stay in our campers or by the pool (our youth programs and youth worship) without realizing the full feast of food and fellowship are at the table where it all comes together.

A few years ago I read a powerful little book called *Youth Ministry 3.0* by Mark Oestreicher.[1] Marko turned me around in my approach to youth ministry through that book. One specific point that had an impact on me was his statement that youth ministry should not be driven by programs but should transform teenagers by being the presence of Christ within the missional community. He spoke of a "communion" of believers that included youth. Then Marko stated that this shift in youth ministry isn't something we can program. It's not a curriculum we can buy and use in our churches. Rather, it's an attitude and an understanding that has to be nurtured and grown in the congregation. Drat! I wanted to start this new focus next week, and I was all ready to buy the handbook.[2]

In the years that followed, I began looking for ways to help congregations focus on that communion that Marko discussed. I've found some things that help, and I've recognized some things we do in youth ministry and in the church that work against such community. I've discovered ways that I "ghettoize" or "silo" my youth ministry (more on this in chapter 1) and how even though such models may boost my youth ministry numbers, these aren't models that bring youth to know and experience the presence of the Christ. Likewise (and perhaps this is even more important) these exclusionary models hold back an experience of God's kingdom from the community of faith.

This book isn't necessarily an attempt at programming the communion that Marko pointed us to. He's right—that can't be done. We can, however, make a change in the direction that youth ministry is heading within our churches and allow that new direction to affect all of our programming—inside our youth ministry as well as in the rest of the church.

Why do we hold back from our young the blessings of gathering and interacting with the whole body? What makes us think it is right to send various parts of the body of Christ away from the food table, each part taking refuge in a separate space? How can we expect our young adults to adapt to church and faith when the first time they experience what it means to be a congregation is when they're out on their own?

In his letter to the Corinthians, Paul makes an analogy about the faith community being like the human body, stating that we are all gifted in different ways and no one part of the body is more important than another. We must all work together, meaning we must interact with each other in order to allow all of the abilities and gifts of the body to function as they are called:

> Now if the foot should say, "Because I am not a hand, I do not belong to the body," it would not for that reason stop being part of the body. And if the ear should say, "Because I am not an eye, I do not belong to the body," it would not for that reason stop being part of the body. If the whole body were an eye, where would the sense of hearing be? If the whole body were an ear, where would the sense of smell be? But in fact God has placed the parts in the body, every one of them, just as he wanted them to be. If they were all one part, where would the

body be? As it is, there are many parts, but one body. (1 Corinthians 12:15-20)

I love how Paul points to the absurdity of one eyeball rolling around, thinking it is not in need of the rest of the body. We understand this—even thousands of years after Paul wrote these words. People in the church recognize God's spiritual gifts and the need to work together with people of different gifts and abilities. I wonder, though, if we are missing another point about the body of Christ. If Paul were to take a look at our churches today—the separate worship services, mission trips, studies, and divisions by age group—he might alter his body absurdity into something like this:

> Now if the foot should say, "Because I am not a hand, I need to carry out all my actions with other feet," it would not for that reason stop being part of the body. And if the ear should say, "Because I am not an eye, I must only gather with the other ears," it would not for that reason stop being part of the body. If the eyes were to spend time only with 20 or 30 other eyes, how would they know how to work with the hands? If the 50 ears were to say, "Because there are so many of us, we do not need to function with the nose or the mouth," how would they understand the total workings of the body? But in fact God has placed the parts in the body, every one of them, just as he wanted them to be. If all the parts only worked in seclusion with their own kind, how would the body function as one? As it is, there are many parts that must take note and insight from each other, forming one body.[3]

I am willing to stand at the front of the line of those who've supported this silo mind-set in the past. For much of the time that I've been serving as a professional youth minister in the church, I could build a youth ministry silo strong and secure enough to bring up youth with a faith that seemed solid and sustainable. I've discovered, though, (thanks to connections made over social media) that over half of the many youth who came through my youth ministry programming are no longer active in a church in their adulthood.

Statistics tell us that people whose teenage church experiences were limited to youth rooms and youth worship, lock-ins and mission trips, fundraisers and spiritual retreats, and who never got to know the whole church in the form of corporate worship, nursery and music ministries, fellowship dinners and planning meetings—the time spent together as one body—will grow up continually searching for a church that is like their youth ministry experience. They won't know what to look for in a church; they won't have a faith that is nurtured by the stories and the lives of the whole body of Christ. Youth need to hear the stories, to be a part of the body, to recognize how they fit into the community.

Much of my understanding and encouragement regarding the topic of integrating youth into the life of the whole congregation comes from the words and research of Fuller Youth Institute's Sticky Faith, and especially from The Youth Cartel's Youth Ministry Coaching Program. After about 25 years of doing youth ministry in the local church, I'd begun to wonder if I should switch tracks and agree to serve as a pastor of a church. It seemed like I'd either hit a brick wall or something was lacking in my youth ministry.

I picked up *Youth Ministry 3.0* around that time, and it reshaped my focus on youth ministry. I began to get excited about helping youth become a part of the community, rather than being just another individual in a separate program. Shortly after that, I heard Kara Powell speak at the National Youth Workers Convention. Tie that in with a sit-down lunch with Mark DeVries during that same conference, and I was off

and running to start something new in my approach to youth ministry.

In this book you will discover how the church (and specifically youth ministry) has found itself so separated in its ministries and relationships, why so many continue to function this way, and why it's our calling as the church to bring our youth into a connection with others. You'll also read about people and communities that have been blessed by an integration of youth with the entire congregation. I hope these examples and practical suggestions will be more than just programs you can implement into your own church. Make them springboards to new, vital relationships that add stories, fellowship, and foundation to the life of your congregational gatherings.

# CHAPTER 1
# BRING THEM IN FROM THE SILO: WHY IS INTEGRATION IMPORTANT?

*Why did the denominations of the Protestant mainline give up on a commitment to education at the heart of their liturgies of infant baptism or dedication?*
— Charles R. Foster, *Generation to Generation*

Growing up in the Dakotas, I was accustomed to seeing lots of silos. A silo is a storage building (usually tall and cylindrical) where grain is kept on a farm. As my family and I drove along the Dakota highways, I could look out and recognize a thriving farm. It would have the main farmhouse and a number of side buildings—a barn or two where animals and equipment were kept, and a few silos where grain was held for selling or for feeding the livestock.

When I was 15 and moved to suburban Atlanta, I began to get involved in the youth ministry at the little church down the road. This was new to me. In North Dakota the closest thing

©iStockphoto.com/steverts

21

to youth ministry that I'd experienced was the occasional teen dance that was held at the Presbyterian and Catholic churches in town. I hadn't expected that people my age would willingly (and excitedly) go to church for lessons, discussions, games, and, yes, every now and then there were some dances. The part that really hit me, though, was that many of these churches in our Metro Atlanta area had separate spaces—whole buildings—dedicated to youth ministry. As we drove by a church, I could see what appeared to be thriving churches. They had a main building (containing the sanctuary) and some side buildings—an educational building, a gym, and sometimes a separate youth building.

It strikes me today that these separate "silos" of ministry may not have been a sign of a thriving church—at least not by some standards. A farm with numerous silos showed that things were going well. After all, a farmer wants to sell as much grain as possible. Storing up the grain is essential until it's ready to go to the market (or wherever farmers send their grain). Storing grain in a silo keeps it safe and dry, holding off decay and keeping it securely away from animals or those who would devour and steal. You'd never store grain in the main house, though. That's where the family lived. That's where life was nurtured. That's where the grain was eventually cooked and eaten, becoming something that nourished a family. (I know, much of the grain is also fed to the farm animals. This is an analogy, folks, so go with it.)

So why would we think that having separate silos of ministry would help things thrive within the church family? Why would we think that keeping ministries and groups of people separate would be the best way to nurture the faith family? For a church to be nurtured, we must allow the various ages and stories to interact by integrating the community. We certainly aren't wishing to sell our youth as grain—moving them away from the community of faith—and yet, that's exactly what's happening when we choose to model our youth ministry (and other ministries in the church) as separate silos on a farm. Eventually many who've grown up in the silo of youth ministry leave the farm.

How did youth ministry begin to splinter off like this, choosing (or allowing itself) to become separate from the rest of the congregation? What are some of the cultural and historical models and values that helped keep our youth out of the main house?

Understand that I'm not suggesting that churches disband their youth ministries. The youth ministry is not at fault for separating the youth from the congregation. I'm also not suggesting that all youth ministries with a separate youth space—a building, wing, or room—are silos. Rather, we're using this image of the church with the separate buildings to point to an internal structure that exists in many of our churches and in the minds of our church members—one where the splintering and dividing of ministries (especially age groups) is not only allowable, but often pursued. Let's look at how this model became so accepted.

It's hard to comprehend growing up in a culture where most of the people you associate with each day are a different age and generation than your own. That's the way it would have been before the emergence and popularity of public school, though. By the 1950s, teenagers were expected to be in school each day of the school year, and they were rubbing elbows and exchanging ideas and dreams with their peers most of the waking day. Now more than 60 years later, youth have become comfortable being separated from the rest of the family and community for much of their day.

This separation hasn't been limited to public school, though. Churches also developed age-level classes for teaching faith

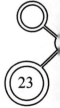

and developing community. In fact, it is the Sunday school system that gave birth to the public schools. As early as the late 1800s, churches began Sunday schools for various age levels, and then in the early 1900s, public schools began recognizing the importance of dividing students by grade. (My first public school experience in the small South Dakota town where I grew up in the mid-1960s was a combined class of first through fourth grades.)

Summer camp experiences and camp meeting times in churches also seemed successful in faith development for teenagers. As denominations took seriously their vow and call to raise children in a Christian community, they intentionally developed curriculum and guidelines for educating their children through each stage of faith.

Like public education, faith education for youth became a more intentional process. Charles Foster, a Christian educator since the 1960s and author of *From Generation to Generation: The Adaptive Challenge of Mainline Protestant Education in Forming Faith*, takes us back to the way churches conscientiously raised their children in the faith:

> A little girl in a congregation would probably have begun participating regularly in the worship life of the congregation before she turned five. When she entered first grade she could join the youngest of the children's choirs and begin rehearsing ways to participate in congregational worship. Here she would learn some of the hymns of the church and during an expanded Wednesday afternoon session explore in greater depth some of the Bible stories she was encountering in the Sunday church school. Because the pastors visited the full range of Sunday school classes, taught in Vacation Church School, and may have been in their home, her parents would have assumed she would, like the older

children in the church, view them as friends. Since they had been taking her to church fellowship dinners since she was a small baby, they would undoubtedly assume she knew people in the church of all ages and that many of her closest friends in the years ahead would be from church. … She would move on to the junior high class…and then senior high youth fellowships…with their mission projects, retreats, study, and extensive involvement in district and conference youth activities and camping programs.[4]

Foster goes on to describe how this young lady's church may very likely send her name to some of the college campuses that are run by her denomination and be invited by the college ministries at those campuses to come visit. He states that one would find similar goals and structures in all the mainline denominations (as well as a few differences), and that all shared "a common intent for their education to facilitate the eventual identification of their children with their traditions of faith."[5]

Some mainline denominations started focusing specifically on youth ministries even in the early 1950s. The Methodist Church (later the United Methodist Church) had Methodist Youth Fellowship as early as 1941—the result of merging the earlier youth groups of the Methodist Protestant Church and the Methodist Episcopal Church. Those youth ministries originated in the late 1800s. However, these early youth ministries were not very directed toward youth outside the church. It would take the parachurch ministries of Young Life and Youth for Christ to help churches recognize the importance of reaching beyond their doors to teenagers in the community.

With their focus on outreach and evangelism, Young Life and Youth for Christ helped churches to view youth ministry as an avenue to draw teenagers into the life of the church. Youth for

Christ and Young Life reached teens through weekly gatherings that were fun and energetic and contained some portion of a gospel message. If the organization really functioned the way it was supposed to, it also pointed kids in the direction of a local congregation to get them plugged into ministries there. The activities and energy from these gatherings pointed denominations to some new and exciting ways to attract youth—ways that were different from the normal "church" way of doing ministry.

So it was only natural that local churches began copying some of the Youth for Christ practices of reaching out to and bringing in teenagers from the community. After all, if a teen was interested in the way they did things at Young Life (or even at summer camp) then, "Let's have similar things for teenagers here at our church!"

Adding youth ministry programs in the 1950s and 1960s meant finding people who would spend a bit more time with the youth—people who would connect with the teenage world and yet also draw youth to the gospel of Jesus Christ. These first gatherings were based on spreading the word and speaking the gospel to youth in ways they could understand. Youth gatherings in churches usually consisted of a sanctuary space or a large room with chairs arranged in rows and a front space with a lectern or maybe even a stage. A skit or stunt might draw people in, then some singing of youth-oriented Christian hymns or camp songs (still before the days of "Kum Ba Yah," we're talking "Nothing but the Blood" and "I'll Fly Away"), followed by the main speaker—someone who could communicate the gospel to teenagers. (Youth ministry was, for the most part, about preaching to teenagers.)[6]

As youth ministry activities became more popular, teenagers began going to youth group more often than they went to "regular church." However, churches were naïve as to how their own actions and youth outreach ministries were keeping young people from their pews. When it was realized that the young were attending worship or other church-wide activities less and less, the pushback to maintain youth ministry activities became stronger and stronger. ("This is where the teens are attending, so let's go to the youth ministry programs to build their faith and explain to them the importance of coming to church.")

Some took note, though, and saw what was happening in these early stages of splintering and division. In 1965, the World Council of Churches called for an end to these isolated youth ministries programs. Their concern was that these ministries were becoming "ghettoized" and had lost their focus on the main mission of the church.[7] Some churches and denominations answered this call by simply cutting the funding for such ministry or cutting the ministries altogether, but without refocusing on integrating those youth back into the fold, teens either dropped away or ran to the church up the road that still funded their programming.

Churches with youth ministries gained more and more popularity by the late 1970s, and as churches recognized the draw of the games and energy of Youth for Christ and Young Life, churches (especially the bigger ones) started setting aside some space that was designated as the youth space—a room or two that could be decorated with comfortable furniture, a hallway or wing that had Ping-Pong tables and posters, or even a "youth building" where teens could be as noisy as they wanted and not disturb (or be disturbed by) what was happening elsewhere at church. This was when we began dividing the body, sending each group away from the table of the main congregation to exist in its own turf. The popular youth culture of the 1960s and 1970s seemed to scream "rebellion of our youth" and "generation gap," so churches were pleased with anything that kept its teens interested and

involved in church—even if it meant they met in another part of the building. ("Give them space and they'll have a place to hang out.")

It seemed like a great idea. A church that provided a space like this showed that it supported teenagers in the community and valued them so much that it would dedicate its space, budget, and volunteer base to the ministry. The flip side was that it was also moving a vital part of the congregation away from the rest of the family. Not only were the youth given a place to be away, but the adults who offered to take over this program also ended up separated from the rest of the church (at least during youth gatherings).

By the early 1980s, new extracurricular demands took away precious family time, and many committed Sunday school teachers and youth group leaders had rotated out of their roles. The expanding job market for women drew many dedicated teachers into full-time employment, meaning they had less time to teach at church than they once had. Some churches addressed this problem by rotating teachers in and out of classrooms once a month or quarterly. Training for these new volunteers was less available; curriculum lost some of its denominational and traditional connection; and any collaboration of learning between childhood and adolescence happened seldom if at all. "Randomness predominated among teachers, in curriculum, in educational settings, and in the experience of church life in general. Children's choirs, fellowship dinners, even mission and service projects had become programmatic options to be negotiated in the family calendar."[8]

As a result of youth being more involved in school activities and even in youth group programming, their significant relationships with an adult were often limited to a parent (extended family had moved out of the home and, in most cases, out of the same community by the 1970s), a school teacher (only on school grounds), and the youth ministry volunteer. Sometimes coaches would spend time and energy relating to a few kids, but that was often seasonal and could be interpreted by the youth as "because I'm on the team."

Without a significant adult or parent present for most of the day, young people often found themselves completely on their own after school until late in the evenings, and largely invisible to the larger community. As Patricia Hersch notes in *A Tribe Apart: A Journey into the Heart of American Adolescence*, "Adults, burned out by the years of day care arrangements, are happy the kids are old enough to be on their own." In fact, adults often believe teenagers prefer to be left alone. But it seems to Hersch and to many of us who spend time with youth that teenagers are "more isolated and more unsupervised than any other generation," creating what Hersch calls a "tribe apart."[9]

As youth ministry programs became more involved and began to involve more youth, the programming drew youth away from the rest of church activity. No longer was the youth Bible study seen as a side dish to the main course in the sanctuary. By the early 1990s, whatever was happening in the youth group was the main thing for youth, and since then, many youth go to a particular church because of the youth ministry, and they often haven't even been to a worship service in the main building or interacted with the rest of the congregation.

I wonder how surprised the leaders of the early church would be if they were to have a conversation with a teenager who is active in a church's youth ministry today:

> "I'm so glad to hear that you're learning about the Christian faith through a church home."

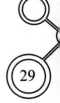

"Yes, I enjoy going to youth group and relating to my friends there on a faith level. Worship and service have become very important to me."

"You say youth group, but do you also have friends at church who are older than you who can guide you in the faith as they have been guided?"

"I know a few adults. They teach my class and go on retreats with the youth group."

"What about the other adults who worship with you weekly? Do you know many of them personally?"

"I go to the youth worship. Every now and then we lead worship in the sanctuary, but each week my parents drop me off at the youth room where I worship with other teenagers. I guess I get to the sanctuary on Easter and Christmas Eve, when we don't have youth worship."

"Wait. Where do you find support and help? Who teaches you trust and hope through trial? How do you serve each other if you aren't with them?"

"I do all that—with the other youth my age."

A church thrives on relationships—with God, with its leadership, and with each other. Relationships need interaction and communication. A church also thrives on interconnectedness and a certain synergy of faith—ways for various experiences between people to feed and nurture each other's faith. That's hard to do when there are separate ministries that never seem to connect. A farm doesn't wish to blend the corn with the soybeans (thus, the silos). But a church must draw from all ministries, and a congregation experiences the kingdom of God when it blends and mixes all of God's people.

A ministry of service or of hospitality learns from the needs of the young and the old; a ministry of worship must draw on the connectedness of everyone in order to recognize and celebrate what it means to be the body of Christ. In the words of Paul:

> As it is, there are many parts, but one body. The eye cannot say to the hand, "I don't need you!" And the head cannot say to the feet, "I don't need you." On the contrary, those parts of the body that seem to be weaker are indispensable, and the parts that we think are less honorable we treat with special honor. And the parts that are unpresentable are treated with special modesty, while our presentable parts need no special treatment. But God has put the body together, giving greater honor to the parts that lacked it, so that there should be no division in the body, but that its parts should have equal concern for each other. (1 Corinthians 12:20-25)

Being satisfied with our young Christians participating only within the silo of youth ministry is akin to an eye or a hand deciding never to work in collaboration with other parts of the body.

A church community thrives on interconnectedness and collaboration because humans thrive on such things. We learn from each other, and the more diverse we are the more we learn. In the faith community this is important, because we learn more about our faith and our traditions from those who have gone before us. Children, youth, adults, men, women, clergy, laity—all help nurture each other's faith and relationship with the body of Christ. For some reason, though, churches have started measuring success in ministry in the same way we might measure the success of a farm. How big and how full is the silo? How many silos are there? How many staff do we have taking care of each silo? If the silo is full, then it must be successful. Time to build a bigger silo and hire more farmhands.

As thriving youth ministries continue to draw people (and draw envy from churches that cannot afford the glitzy youth rooms and expensive electronics) they almost become churches in themselves. "Youth workers clamored to develop youth-y churches-within-churches that were loosely attached to, but functionally separate (and autonomous) from, the church that housed and funded them."[10]

Youth ministry professionals in some churches are hired to "have relationships with teenagers" and "build youth ministry programs that will draw youth from around the community into a relationship with Christ." The youth minister has become the main staff person relating to teens, the adult volunteers are the church members that the youth know, and the youth activities, retreats, mission trips, small groups, lock-ins, and social gatherings become church experience for the youth. In many settings (especially the larger ones—either because of a need for space or to draw in more youth), an alternate worship time and experience has been created specifically for youth so they will connect with church even better—hearing a youth-oriented message and singing youth-oriented songs led by youth-cultured praise bands.

Even though our youth programming brings youth into some sort of church participation, by the time those active youth exit the silo (when they turn 18 or graduate from high school, in most cases), they have no comfort or positive experience with what it means to exist in the mainstream church ministries— the family member would rather stay in the silo than move into the main house. When they start looking for a church as young adults, these former youth know only to look for something akin to their youth group.

# CHAPTER 2
# THE DANGERS OF PLAYING THE NUMBERS GAME

*Large is part of the value system of Youth*
*Ministry 2.0; small is a cornerstone to Youth*
*Ministry 3.0. Communion necessitates small.*
*Contextualization begs for small. Discernment*
*requires small. Mission is lived out in small.*
— Mark Oestreicher, *Youth Ministry 3.0*

For years I found myself on a Sunday night looking out over the youth group and counting how many had come that night. If the numbers were pretty similar to the way it had been in the past few weeks, we were staying steady. If the numbers were significantly less than they had been the last few weeks, then we were slipping. But if the count was higher than it had been the last month or more, then in my mind (and the mind of my senior pastor and church leaders) we were successful.

The question I should have asked myself, though, is this: *Successful in what?*

If the goal was to increase the numbers from the last few weeks then, yes, we were successful. If the goal was to make the other bean counters in the church pleased then, yes, we were successful. But somewhere in the corners of my youth-ministry brain, I knew that counting was not the way to determine success. Why was I less confident and more frustrated at the effectiveness of my ministry when I had an evening of 300+ youth than on the nights when I met with a handful? The problem was that I didn't have a better way of measuring our success. I remember one evening in particular when there were over 350 youth present—which was a great turnout—and yet I felt very little like a minister and more like an activities director. I was frustrated at not being able to connect many of that crowd with those who could help make their faith meaningful—the adult volunteers, a congregation that cared for them, and especially Jesus.

For many, the way to determine if a program in youth ministry is successful is by how many people show up. It's been this way for years—at least it's this way on Monday morning in the staff meeting and at youth ministry gatherings when you introduce yourself to a new group of youth leaders and try to tell them about your youth group. This may be because our boss or the supervising committee or the parent group or the head usher on Sunday morning ask us, "How many did you have at youth group last week?" or it may be because we connect coming to the youth program with coming to Christ. Neither of these, though, are good reasons to use numbers as a determinate of success.

When youth pastor Doug Fields was interviewed by Pastor Rick Warren and the church leadership of Saddleback Church, he told Warren that it would take five years before any sign of fruitfulness would be evident from his youth ministry leadership. (And that's only a sign of fruitfulness—not the full harvest.)[11] Such wise insight from Fields; such patient leadership from Warren.

Reliance on numbers is an easy trap to fall into, though. Throughout the years of its existence, the success of a youth ministry has seemed to rest on how fast it is growing. If a new youth minister arrives at a church and numbers plummet within the first six months, people soon ask where things have gone wrong. Something must be wrong if people have quit coming, right? On the other hand, if attendance rises 5 or 10 percent in the first six months, then many would say that something is working right. Parents and church leaders would likely attribute the change to the new youth leadership. It's possible that fewer are showing up because a more in-depth study has begun or because there is more of an emphasis on worship and testimony. Likewise, it's possible that more are coming because the program has moved to one of glitz and entertainment with very little content. Is one model worse than another? Not always. Each model of ministry is weighed according to the context and timing.

Willow Creek Church, in the Chicago area, went through amazing growth in attendance and, more specifically, youth ministry numbers since the 1980s. For years they looked at those numbers and determined that what they were doing was successful. The mission of the ministries of Willow Creek was to help people become fully developed followers of Jesus Christ. In order to determine if they had, in fact, become successful in achieving their mission, Willow Creek decided to check up on those who had been through their ministry, embarking on a multi-year qualitative study of its ministry.

Willow Creek was surprised at what they found.

For Willow Creek, program participation was always important. The church believed that more participation in programs led to more people becoming disciples of Jesus Christ. Having put so much emphasis into this program-driven model, you can understand their shock when the research revealed that "Increasing levels of participation in these sets of activities does NOT predict whether someone's becoming more of a disciple of Christ. It does NOT predict whether they love

God more or they love people more."

Senior Pastor Bill Hybels summarized the findings this way:

> Some of the stuff that we have put millions of dollars into thinking it would really help our people grow and develop spiritually, when the data actually came back, it wasn't helping people that much. Other things that we didn't put that much money into and didn't put much staff against is stuff our people are crying out for.[12]

Other research has helped define success in the area of youth ministry. LifeWay Research conducted a survey in April of 2007 of more than 1,000 adults ages 18 to 30. The survey results revealed that two-thirds of young adults who attend a church for at least a year in high school will stop attending for at least a year in their young adult years. Related to the findings, Brad Waggoner, vice president of research and ministry development at LifeWay, stated,

> Relationships are often the glue that keep people in church or serve as the attraction to begin attending again following a period of absenteeism. Many people are deeply influenced by friends and loved ones…Frequent and intentional contact (between church members and youth and young adults) can either prevent or counteract the tendency of some to drop out of church.[13]

Twenty percent of those surveyed who'd left the church stated that the main reason for leaving was because they "didn't feel connected to the people in my church."

Kara Powell references the LifeWay research as well as her research through Fuller Youth Institute and its four-year College Transition Project (CTP) to understand what that transition from high school to college was like and to identify steps that parents and leaders can take to encourage in kids a faith that lasts (what Fuller calls "sticky faith"). Powell's research and the resource and ministries that followed, discovered that even though awareness of the importance of high school ministries is increasing, 40 to 50 percent of youth group graduates drift from God and from the church after high school.[14]

There is a difference between short-term success and long-term success, and long-term success is really what we want to know in order to determine if a ministry is effective, isn't it? We youth ministers have a student for, at most, six or so years under our youth ministry umbrella. Even if an individual is able to stay involved in the church after graduating high school, the relationship to the youth ministry changes. We want church experience and relationships during the youth years to nurture faith in such a way that something fruitful and sustainable will result. Simply having youth who are excited about what you're doing in youth group is not necessarily going to grow a fruitful faith. That's because short-term success has to do with getting somewhere fast—usually at the cost of something else; long-term success has more to do with sustainability.

If a youth ministry (or any ministry) is sustainable, it means that it can continue through the storm—through hard times, through crises, through moves and transitions of members and leadership, and especially through the "storms of life," also known as adolescence. Long-term success always requires investment, time, and patience. Long-term success in youth ministry means that when individuals are no longer in youth ministry, they still have roots and connections that continue to feed their faith into adulthood.

When I think about long-term success in youth ministry, I'm reminded of Jesus' explanation of the importance of deep roots in the parable of the sower. Here's how he explains the parable to his disciples:

> When anyone hears the message about the kingdom and does not understand it, the evil one comes and snatches away what was sown in their heart. This is the seed sown along the path. The seed falling on rocky ground refers to someone who hears the word and at once receives it with joy. But since they have no root, they last only a short time. When trouble or persecution comes because of the word, they quickly fall away. The seed falling among the thorns refers to someone who hears the word, but the worries of this life and the deceitfulness of wealth choke the word, making it unfruitful. But the seed falling on good soil refers to someone who hears the word and understands it. This is the one who produces a crop, yielding a hundred, sixty or thirty times what was sown. (Matthew 13:19-23)

Having a glitzy youth ministry program that works to get kids to come regularly to youth group but doesn't work on deep, lasting relationships with the body of Christ is similar to sowing seeds on rocky ground. Too often we raise youth in our youth ministry silos who hear the Word of God or experience the great worship or powerful discussion or even enjoy the meaningful mission trip and "at once receives it with joy. But since they have no root, they last only a short time. When trouble or persecution comes because of the word, they quickly fall away." If we are to believe the statistics from Fuller Youth Institute, LifeWay, Willow Creek, and some of the mainline denominations, many churches are allowing seeds to fall on the rocky soil, putting forth shallow roots that fall away when students leave high school.

Mark DeVries, author of *Sustainable Youth Ministry*, writes, "Building a sustainable, thriving youth ministry is not only possible, it's actually predictable. Sadly, most churches don't have the patience to wait to build a sustainable youth ministry."[15]

So, how do we know if what we're doing in youth ministry is sustainable and successful? How does one know if the seeds planted will germinate and bear fruit? How do you determine the long-term impact of a message given or the results of a discussion you've had or the effect of an entire Bible study on a youth?

Well, that depends on the target. If the target is short-ranged, like average weekly numbers, attendees on a retreat, who we reach at a local school, how many heard my plea to serve, or those who commit to Christ in a year, then you can measure success through your tally sheet.

But if your target is to help teenagers become adult disciples of Jesus Christ and to make sure that what is learned on those retreats and mission trips and Bible studies and connections with God will be nurtured and confirmed over and over again into adulthood, then you'll have to use something else to determine the effectiveness or sustainability of your ministry.

Truly significant impact and success of a youth ministry means finding out if those who participated continue to remain involved in ministry and discipleship in their adulthood. Did the teachings about serving others follow into adult lives of service? Are the youth active in a church later as young adults? Do they still concentrate on being disciples of Jesus Christ? What kinds of relationships do they have with church members now that they are no longer in the youth ministry? How many are still only involved in youth ministry as an adult?

Measuring this kind of success means it could be years or even decades before we know the impact and sustainability of our ministry. That's too long for you or your youth ministry leadership team to know if what's happening is effective or successful. By the time you find out that something didn't work, generations of youth will have gone through your program. Rather, let's take a look at what kinds of things have the highest success rates at keeping individuals connected to the church and to their Christian faith. There is already some helpful research out there that tells us what has (and hasn't) been effective in keeping people connected to the church and to God. Following in this chapter are some of the most effective and successful church practices that correlate with positive connection to God and to the church even after someone leaves high school.

At first glance, it may appear that this overview lacks any kind of teaching or educational model. Recognize, though, that the values and correlations in this list can be incorporated into various curricula, classrooms, and retreats as well as the day-to-day functions of church life and ministry. The key is going to be finding ways to help your congregation make the shift in its ideals and practices.

## WORSHIP

The Sticky Faith people at Fuller Youth Institute (FYI) wanted to find out what kinds of ministries had the most positive outcome on preparing youth for their transition into adulthood. They took a look at the young adults who were still active in a church after graduation and tried to find out the kinds of ministries they were involved in as teenagers in their churches.

Fuller discovered that those young adults who were involved as teenagers in areas beyond the youth ministry programs in their churches—singing in the church choir, participating in intergenerational worship, leadership in church committees, helping in the nursery—were more likely to be involved in a church when they became adults. Even more specifically, when FYI looked to see what most of these who had stuck with the church had in common, it wasn't that they were involved in their church's youth ministry; it wasn't that they went on mission trips or even worked at Vacation Bible School each year with the rest of their youth group. The single most common activity that young adults had experienced in their churches as teenagers that seemed to help their faith roots grow deep and also helped them remain active in a church as adults was worship—and not youth worship, either. It was combined, corporate, intergenerational worship.[16]

When the body of believers gathers in one place and brings prayers and responses together before God, something holy happens. Traditions and rituals and our stories play an integral part in our faith development, but when we cut our youth out of that practice or remove our children from such an experience, we are ending the tradition and ritually shutting the door on helping our young grow into being a part of the larger community. Granted, it may look like having a youth worship service at the same time as the main worship service will get more teenagers to church and help them hear the gospel, but intergenerational worship is the most bonding activity that a community can do together. And if our youth don't know what it feels like to worship with a community of people of all ages, then they will be lost when they are no longer in youth group.[17]

This isn't to say that your youth ministry cannot be effective if you have a youth worship service that is separate from the main worship service in the sanctuary. God shows up regardless of where we worship. But when we remove youth (or any specific age group) from the worship experience, we are taking away the most effective thing that ties youth to the body. There are other ways to help keep that bond strong, but you'll have to work twice (or three times) as hard and do it much more intentionally.

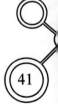

41

I met recently with a 20-year youth ministry veteran. He's been in his current church for over 15 years and has a pretty substantial youth ministry program based on solid education and significant relationships with adults. A recent concern has been some of the pressure he's received from youth and parents to have a youth worship service running concurrently with the main (highly traditional) worship service. There is no "modern" or "contemporary" worship available at the church, and many see nearby megachurches that offer high-energy youth worship on Sunday mornings and believe their church should offer the same.

The interesting thing about traditional worship services at this church is that the youth regularly sit in the front pews. The whole congregation is aware of the participation of youth in the worshiping community, and the youth enjoy their senior pastor's messages. They connect well with the community through its worshiping traditions. It's a strength. To offer a substitute for what they already do well would only take away from something that is working. Ministry should never be thought of as a competition with other communities of faith. Help your parents and youth recognize how their community—their family of faith—is the best one for them to allow their seeds of faith to push deep into good soil.

## FAITH CONNECTIONS WITH SIGNIFICANT ADULTS

One of the reasons intergenerational, mixed worship is so effective in connecting youth into the life of the whole church is that it places them into a faith connection with adults—people in the faith who have some experience in their relationship with Christ. Youth who have strong faith in Christ usually have good relationships with significant adults who are also strong in their faith.

I recently heard a story from Mike Park, the student integration pastor at Newsong Church in Irvine, California. Mike shared about a boy in his church, we'll call him Jeff, who attended a summer camp for people who had family members with cancer. At that camp Jeff met Carl (again, not his real name), an older gentleman who had volunteered to serve for a short while at camp. Jeff and Carl really connected one summer during that camp experience—so much so that Carl decided to become a regular staff member at the camp, and Jeff continued to keep in touch with Carl.

Jeff's dad recognized the strength of his son's relationship with Carl, and years later he invited Carl to a graduation party that he'd organized for his son. This was a special kind of graduation party. Jeff's father invited five adults to dinner— Christian men whom he could see had played an important role in his son's life. At one point in the evening, each one was asked to read a blessing and offer encouragement to Jeff, the graduate. It was a powerful evening as this father witnessed how God was using these significant adults in Jeff's life to mold and mentor him into becoming a devoted Christian adult.

I love that Carl, who wasn't a member of Jeff's family, wasn't a nearby neighbor, and didn't even go to Jeff's church, was one of the most influential relationships in Jeff's Christian journey. Carl acted out his Christian calling of raising the young into the "way that leads to life eternal," and his continued relationship with Jeff is a wonderful example of the greater church and how we are all connected.

## PARENTS
Of all the influential adults at Jeff's graduation dinner, it was Jeff's father who had the most impact. With insight, compassion, and confidence, Jeff's dad allowed other men to influence his son's faith upbringing.

Fuller Institute's Sticky Faith research discovered that parents have the strongest effect on a teenager's faith. We can connect youth to a youth minister, get them involved in a small group led by a dynamic Christian adult leader, and make sure our teens are at church every Sunday listening to the sermon, but the parental relationship will still be the most significant one in the life of a teen.

I've heard parents sometimes back off from influencing their children's faith by letting them decide whether or not to go to church or participate in ministries at some time in their teenage years. These parents want to "give the child a choice" or "not influence him with my own beliefs." All this silence does, though, is very loudly tell the child that faith must not be all that important to the parent—still imprinting on that child some strong responses when it comes to faith development.

A parent who recognizes his or her influence on the child's faith will begin looking for support in this role. Who better to help those parents influence their children's faith than their own peers—other parents of teens and other adults who share a concern for and commitment to the children being raised in the faith community? What better place to find such peers and interested adults who recognize the importance of faith than in one's church? Who better to help a parent raise a child in faith than those who verbalize it in a public promise before God?

This knowledge of faith development can help direct the actions and energy of youth ministry professionals (and volunteers) as well. If a parent is the most influential relationship in the faith of a teenager, then it seems likely that spending more time empowering and informing parents in faith-related topics and adolescent faith development would show great results for our efforts. Help your youth ministry team focus on relationships among the parents of your youth and children, bringing support and encouragement into the structure of the faith community.

## FAMILIARITY WITH CHURCH (IN BOTH DIRECTIONS)

Building a familiarity between your youth and the adults in your church is a two-way street. The task of the youth minister includes being a champion for your teenagers to the adults in your community. Help the entire congregation feel comfortable sitting next to the youth, or inviting them into the chancel choir; make sure your youth who show potential as leaders aren't overlooked when people are nominated for boards or committees. The more familiar we are with each other, the more we'll recognize when people are missing—and the harder we'll work to try to keep them involved.

Perhaps one reason so many youth who participate in ministries outside the youth programming (like the nursery, chancel choir, regular worship service, and church-wide dinners) stick with the church into adulthood is because they are already familiar with how things work outside the youth silo. Those youth who seem most comfortable in your youth ministry but have never built relationships elsewhere in the church may very well be the first to leave once they discover and experience unfamiliarity for the first time.

## A TIME AND A PLACE TO LEAD (AND TO FAIL)

It seems obvious now that if we're going to train our youth to become leaders in the community of faith, then we need to stand alongside them as they slowly begin to lead in the ministries of the whole congregation. Our young need to feel united not only while they're sitting in worship among believers of all ages, but also experiencing the joys (and frustrations) of leading worship, participating in planning

meetings, serving in church-wide local outreach and community service, and, yes, even attending committee meetings.

The youth minister should be a champion for the youth in times of leadership development—and this leadership should stretch beyond the youth ministry committees and teams. Become "that person" who is always pushing to place youth into every committee in the church. The worst thing that could happen is the congregation will see you as someone who wants youth involved in church-wide leadership.

The United Methodist Church and other denominations require in their bylaws that a youth or young adult serve on some of the most influential committees. However, many churches don't push for this. That may be because we often hire youth ministers from outside our own denomination—not always a bad thing, but it can mean that the youth minister isn't aware of how the denomination already views youth in the church. If your denomination expects youth to be involved in certain leadership positions, then push the envelope and get them involved. If it does not, then encourage leadership to bring some of your young leaders alongside them as "shadows" who are learning for a time what it means to lead.

## PRACTICE LEARNING

As youth ministers, we seek to help youth learn in ways that foster faith—encouraging various experiences and understandings that encounter the creative and redemptive work of God. Chuck Foster calls it "learning that cultivates the vitality of the relationship of congregations and their members to the God who calls them into community."[18]

That kind of learning cannot be left to chance, says Foster. It must be practiced over and over again through the community of faith. "Practice learning" emphasizes participation as children accept the coaching of a mentor, parent, or teacher through intentional repetitions. Repeating faith tasks may sound boring (after all, it is "repetitious"), but it's always been a key part of faith education and development.

Take, for example, the story of Moses as he directs the Israelites to recite the Commandments over and over again, to talk about them at home and in their journeys, and to write them on their doorposts.

> Fix these words of mine in your hearts and minds; tie them as symbols on your hands and bind them on your foreheads. Teach them to your children, talking about them when you sit at home and when you walk along the road, when you lie down and when you get up. Write them on the doorframes of your houses and on your gates, so that your days and the days of your children may be many in the land the LORD swore to give your ancestors, as many as the days that the heavens are above the earth. (Deuteronomy 11:18-21)

Likewise, Moses' instructions around the Passover meal call us to teach through practice learning. (See Deuteronomy 16.) Moses really did have some great examples of being an educator.

As children repeat a practice over and over again "they begin to develop the confidence for ever more competent participation in the community of these conversations."[19] The more a youth hears and sees people he or she knows talk about and practice the faith, the more confident and comfortable he or she feels in being a participant of the community.

Another example of practice learning is in singing hymns or songs of faith. When singing songs over and over again (especially diverse songs—old hymns as well as gospel songs and including contemporary or modern praise songs), we begin articulating our faith story. At first it may be only words on a page or screen, but over time participation in this worship tradition connects us to Scripture, doctrine, and tradition, teaching us as we speak and sing and dwell on the words coming from our mouths.

Singing is only one way practice learning strengthens a person's bond to the community of faith. Start using practice learning in conversations about beliefs and doctrines, in committee meetings, offering prayers, in caring for the sick and serving the homeless, and most importantly in the reading of Scripture and our liturgies.

## EXPERIENCE OF SHARING FAITH AND STORIES

One of the best ways to encourage youth in their faith development is giving them the freedom to speak ideas and ask questions out loud about faith and theology. Youth who can verbalize their faith with others are more likely to have an owned faith and one that integrates with their everyday life. The church should be the safe place for that to happen.

A teenager needs to know that he or she can speak out or offer ideas and not be criticized or shot down when others don't agree. Granted, this kind of safety can be found in a youth ministry silo, but when others in the church community offer such grace and freedom, those places and those people become safe and appreciated as well. Opening the safety boundaries so they include the entire congregation is one of the best things youth ministry can do for sustainable faith and deep faith roots.

Justin, who grew up in my youth group around 10 years ago,

reflects on something that happened to him when he was nine that, in his perspective, stopped him from ever growing in his faith:

I lost my faith when I was nine years old. It was October. Every bit of involvement I have had with the church has been an attempt, mostly for my mother's sake, to give it a chance. Each time, I have seen a version of what I saw and what disturbed me so much when I was nine.

A series of honest questions were met with varying degrees of punishment by all but one of the people I asked for answers. They were perfectly innocent questions, but the people I spoke to at school, in my family, at church, and eventually in a shrink's office— literally everybody but my physician responded to my questions as if they were what I came to understand as blasphemy.

I know it probably sounds pretty stupid now. But I was nine, so think about it from my perspective. I "knew" something about the universe and, more importantly, I had a prodigiously good understanding of why I knew what I knew for my age. That experience reinforced in me the idea that I might be punished arbitrarily and in a way I can neither understand nor defend myself from for nothing more than being able to explain carbon deterioration. I felt surrounded and scared, especially surrounded. I'm not scared anymore, but I'm still pretty surrounded; and I've not stopped being alone ever since. My consciousness felt like it was brutally severed from my fellow man by that experience. Sometimes I feel like a cornered animal; sometimes cornered by animals.

— Justin, age 27

Give youth and children opportunities and encouragement to voice personal faith stories and talk openly about their own beliefs. It's vital that young Christians be unafraid to speak their beliefs out loud, never fearing they might be scolded for "getting it wrong" or for doubting elements others might consider fundamental to their own faith. Youth need time to process what, how, and why they believe. They are just beginning to experience abstract thinking. It's new to them.

They need practice thinking and stating their beliefs. Have you ever tried to understand your own belief about an issue by speaking it out loud, or have you heard someone say, "I just need to hear myself think through this"? Youth need to hear themselves think about the implications of their theology and how it applies to their life experiences.

Dr. Amanda Drury is an assistant professor of practical theology at Indiana Wesleyan University, and author of *Speechless: The Importance of Testifying in Passing on Adolescent Faith* (InterVarsity Press). Dr. Drury says it isn't enough that our faith has only vague beliefs rolling around in our heads. Rather, "We often have to speak what it is we believe in order for that belief to form us." Words have power, and if they're our words, spoken by us, they have even more power. It is very difficult for youth to believe in something they cannot talk about. When the church becomes a safe place where youth can explore what they believe by talking out loud about their beliefs, their questions, their frustrations and joys, and even their doubts, then youth will grow stronger in their faith as well as in their relationship with that faith community.[20]

Drury explains that every linguist and foreign language student believes the best way to learn a language is through immersion experiences. Go live in a village in Mexico for a month and you will learn more Spanish than you would in a whole year of Spanish class. Drury points out that the church community should be an immersion experience for our children and youth (and anyone else of any age who is wishing to learn about the Christian faith). Rather than being content with age-level divisions that tend to silo and even ghettoize our young, we must give teenagers the experiences of voicing their faith within the community.

This kind of permission to openly talk about one's faith can sometimes be difficult for church leaders and small group leaders. How should we respond when we hear a student say, "I strongly believe in reincarnation," or "I'm not so sure that Jesus is God in the flesh"? Watching our young begin to walk down a path that potentially leads away from Christianity is scary. And if we are taking our calling of raising our young in the faith seriously, then our first response is to pull a leash and redirect them on the right path. How we respond and redirect is vital, though. There are far better ways of responding to a youth who is interested in strange pathways than yanking a leash and immediately telling him or her, "We don't ask those questions," or "That isn't Christian."

Help the adults in the church see how they might make themselves available to someone who is exploring other paths. What would happen if a mentor were to walk that path alongside a youth, responding to foreign doctrine and misdirected attention through a Christian lens? Help adults know the right questions to ask a wayward youth (not ones that embarrass or demean); read about a topic together; compare the other doctrine with the traditions of Christianity in ways that invite discussion and the sharing of ideas. Help the youth see the glory and strength of our Christian faith—its mercy and grace, its traditions and stories, its directions and community— while also looking at how those strengths are different from these other faiths.

Mark Oestreicher says he's pretty convinced that a youth who shares incorrect beliefs about his or her Christian faith is at a healthier place and is more likely to grow in a personal, owned faith (and community) than one who shares nothing at all.[21] If we walk alongside our young as they travel their faith pathways, our own presence and faith stories will be witness to the presence of Christ and what it truly means to be Christian.

I've seen this kind of sharing and testimony happen many times on youth retreats. On our confirmation retreat for our younger youth, we spend some time helping middle school kids recognize where God has already been present in their lives. We instruct them to make a map of their faith journey. Supplied with newsprint and markers, the youth are asked to map out the turns and straightaways, the potholes and crossroads, the cliffs and downhill stretches of their lives. They make road maps or draw crazy, looping roller coasters with signs that tell of important experiences in their lives. They add crossroads at points of vital decisions or seeming cliffs and dead ends at times of loss and trauma.

Then these youth (most of them for the first time) tell the rest of the group about their life path, explaining the times when they have felt closest (and farthest) away from God. They talk about how their faith has been nurtured, strengthened, or even damaged through the journey so far. The strength of this exercise isn't so much in the insight or story they tell or hear. It's in the process of speaking it out loud to their peers and hearing each other state their faith story. It's also important that the leaders share their stories right alongside these youth. They, too, talk about the things that happened to them in their childhood, and these adults have now started telling their story about how God continues to nurture the seeds that were planted even in their childhood. It's a wonderful testimony to what John Wesley calls *prevenient grace*.

Explaining grace to a middle schooler isn't easy, but it might help to use Wesley's description of the various ways we experience God's grace. Wesley explains that we first encounter God's grace as *prevenient grace*, recognizing that God is involved in and all around our lives, loving and forgiving and blessing us before we even know there is a God and before we even ask for such love. Wesley also uses *justifying grace* and *sanctifying grace*, but we stick to *prevenient grace* with middle school youth for the most part. It's what they can relate to the most, as it's all about what God has been doing with them before they come to their own conclusions about faith.[22]

54

# CHAPTER 3
# THE BODY AT ITS BEST: THE BLESSINGS OF BEING AN INTEGRATED CHURCH

*With God's help, we will so order our lives*
*after the example of Christ that this child,*
*surrounded by steadfast love, may be established*
*in the faith and confirmed and strengthened*
*in the way that leads to life eternal.*
— The Baptismal Covenant,
*United Methodist Hymnal*

Most small groups (especially in youth ministry) are made up of youth and two (preferably two—be safe here) adults who guide the youth in their learning. It's a helpful model, and it usually is effective in intentional discipleship as well as building relationships between the members of the group. Sometimes, though, small groups—when constricted solely to age levels—also add to the silo of youth ministry, keeping it strongly divided from the rest of the congregation.

I love Dr. Kara Powell's description of her church small group. She calls it a messy mixture of ages and experiences. Here's how she describes it in the foreword to Matthew Deprez' book, *Join Generations: Becoming Unashamedly Intergenerational*:

> [In our small group] there is a family in our life stage—with kids in elementary school, middle school, and high school.

There is a family ten years younger—still having babies.

Then there is a married couple—who are both over seventy years old.

It's the best small group I've ever experienced.

It's not the quietest, most orderly, nor most calm. In the middle of lofty discussions about kingdom living, we are often interrupted by a hungry two-year-old or a fifteen-year-old who just remembered a homework assignment she's got to finish by tomorrow. We sometimes have to eat our brownie dessert quickly because it's thirty minutes past the five-year-old's bedtime and he's melting down.

So what makes this small group the best? It's our commitment to Jesus and to each other, and that those commitments extend across generations.

Sure, it's a bit messier than other small groups (and I mean that both figuratively and literally, as our dining room floor after dinner tonight will attest). But it's partly the mess that makes it so good. So normal. So real.[23]

Kara is talking about the blessings of strength and sharing that come with intergenerational interaction. If we are stronger when we are united, then we are strongest when we are united over diverse ages, races, cultures, stories, callings, and experiences. God is involved in each person's life in awesome and powerful ways. And when we share those stories with each other, we gain insight and experience the kingdom.

# THE BODY WORKS TOGETHER
The blessings of an integrated church are many.

Paul describes the church as something that is diverse and varied in its giftedness. He likens the church to a body and tells us that a church functions best when each part of the body recognizes that all parts are essential. No part is more important, and all must work together in order for the body to do what it needs to do. The stomach, when it is hungry, relies on the hand to take the food and put it to the mouth, where it is chewed by the teeth and swallowed by the throat. In order to gain energy and sustenance from that food, the body's internal organs also do their work. When the parts of the body don't work together, the body suffers.

Every time I consider this analogy, I'm reminded of a unique youth activity from the *Ideas Library* published by Youth Specialties. It involves the youth working together, each one playing his or her part in the body. As a group—with everyone blindfolded except the eyes—the body has to move across the room together, open a jar of peanut butter (or jelly, for those groups with peanut allergies), spread it on bread (yes, they should have to open the bag of bread), and eat. The hands must place the sandwich in the mouth. Remember, all are blindfolded except for the eyes. Like many activities found in the *Ideas Library*, it is active and messy, but it always plays a memorable part in kicking off a discussion about working together with our various gifts.

The body of Christ (the church) will thrive only when all parts work together. That doesn't mean the various ministries disappear, though, to all become one main ministry (as in one big eye or a giant hand of Christ). To stick with Paul's metaphor, the eye doesn't say to the hand, "I don't need you" (1 Corinthians 12). Integration of the church means the various ministries are still individual ministries, but, at the same time, relationships and communication connect the various ministry departments, ages and programs, and, most importantly, people.

## THE OLDER DISCIPLES GIVE INSIGHT TO THE YOUNG

We have a calling and duty as Christians to teach our young the details and traditions of our faith. This isn't simply a responsibility of parents, but all the congregation is given the task of bringing children and youth into a better knowledge and understanding of what it means to be a disciple of Jesus Christ. Many denominations have a pledge or vow that is stated by the congregation when a child is baptized, dedicated, or confirmed. Stating the vow out loud helps the congregation recall its responsibility and acknowledges that it is the duty of the entire congregation—as a whole as well as individuals—to care for the child as he or she grows in the community of faith. That's what it means to be a part of the body of Christ.

This congregational accountability is biblical, too. When Moses passed on God's command to the Hebrew people to retell their story over and over again to their children, answering their questions and reminding them not only what happened, but also who and whose they are, he was communicating the responsibility of the faith community. The Passover meal is a perfect example of this, as the youngest at the table is given a list of questions to ask during the meal, "Why do we eat the bitter herbs? Why is this night different from all other nights?" and the head of the table answers with an account straight from Exodus.

Take the example of Eli and Samuel (the story is from 1 Samuel 3). Samuel grew up to be one of the most important judges and leaders of the Old Testament. God used him to anoint Saul and David, the first two kings of the Hebrew people. The Scriptures tell us that God spoke to Samuel and Samuel communicated God's intent to God's people. Before Samuel's faith had matured, though, he was a young boy—a boy who had not heard God's Word but who was serving in the temple. Scripture tells us that one night, when Samuel was asleep in the temple, he heard a voice calling him by name. Thinking it was Eli, the high priest (who was also asleep in the temple), Samuel ran to Eli and asked him what he wanted. Eli said that he had not called and told Samuel to go back to bed. A little later Samuel heard the voice again. Eli assured him that he had not called and told him to return to bed again. A third time Samuel heard a voice calling his name. This time, when he went to Eli, the high priest impressed on Samuel to listen and if he heard the voice again to reply, "Speak, your servant is listening." Eli suggested that it was God talking to Samuel.

The voice was, in fact, God speaking to Samuel, and Samuel benefited from the insight and discernment of his mentor, Eli. Because the older man had experience and knowledge that he could share with the young boy, Samuel was on his way to becoming one of the most holy and influential men of the Old Testament.

Individuals in your congregation have their own personal faith connections with God, and their stories, insights, and experiences, when shared with youth, can help raise Samuels in your church—people through whom God leads God's people.

## THE YOUNG SHOW THE OLD HOW TO ENTER THE KINGDOM

The blessing of integration isn't a one-way street between the old and the young, though. Don't get stuck in the image of just older, experienced Christians handing down faith and understanding to the young. The blessings go both ways. Jesus

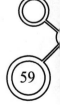

pointed to the little children and said that in order for us all to enter the kingdom of God, we must become as children (Mark 10:13-16).

For a couple years I served as the youth minister of a large—really large—church in Dallas, Texas. We had an active youth and children's ministry, but there were no children or youth in worship. Really. This was before separate youth worship services, but Sunday school went on at the same time as worship, and our congregation had become "one-hour Christians" (as many churches have also done). Parents could drop off their kids at the Sunday school room while they attended worship. I'm not sure who suffered the most from that setup—the children and youth, or the adults. I remember one Sunday, just before Christmas, I was awakened from the slumber of a dull worship service by the beautiful cry of a baby. The baby's wails helped me realize what we adults were missing there in church each Sunday—like the world walking in darkness but awakening to a new light at the coming of the Christ child. The imagery and the symbolism of this on so many levels broke into my Advent worship that morning, and I began to weep.

What better way to be reminded of how we are to become than to surround ourselves with children (and youth) who direct us to the kingdom? When we teach, guide, mentor, laugh, discuss, struggle, and cry with youth as they encounter and search for God in the world, a bit more light shines on the kingdom. Don't limit that to the youth turf of the celebration. That kind of gospel belongs at the food table where everyone is in attendance, drinking in the kingdom through the diverse experiences of everyone there. Our relationship with Christ deepens when we allow ourselves to be the presence of Christ to a child. Through an act of being present with our young, we encounter the incarnation—God present with God's people simply because of love.

# USE IT OR LOSE IT

Jesus told a parable in the Gospel of Matthew (chapter 25) where a king leaves some of his treasures with three servants before leaving on an extended trip. While the king is away, the first two servants invest the money they were given. The third servant, however, only buries his treasure in the dirt, refusing to use it while his master is away.

When the king returns, the first two slaves are able to give back all that they were given and even more, as their investment brought interest. The third servant, after digging up the initial money given to him, returns to the king the original amount—nothing lost, but nothing gained. The money was not used. No risk taken and no investment made.

The king punishes the third servant and divides the money he was given between the first two servants, leaving nothing for the third servant. Jesus ends the parable by saying, "For whoever has will be given more, and they will have an abundance. Whoever does not have, even what they have will be taken from them. And throw that worthless servant outside, into the darkness, where there will be weeping and gnashing of teeth" (Matthew 25:29-30).

What if our youth are part of the talent and treasure that God has given us—has given to our churches? Are we investing those talents in the community? Are we taking the time and energy to include our young in a better experience of what it means to be a part of the whole body? Or are we essentially burying them now so we can dig them up later and hand them back?

The blessing of investment is in the return. The church cannot afford to lose half of its young members because of a lack of investment, yet the king has every right to take away what is

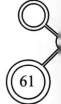

not being invested. Are we setting ourselves up for weeping and gnashing?

## LET EVERYONE COME TO THE TABLE

For me, Communion, or the Lord's Supper, is one of the most powerful traditions of the church. In this sacrament we retell our story, we reclaim our identity, we are renewed and revived in our relationship with God and with each other, and we reconnect with Christ and the understanding that we are all one body. This has been taught to me since I was a child. My parents took me to Communion even before I understood or experienced its power on my life and in the life of the congregation. If I had not encountered Christ's table as a whole community (but only in children's church or on a youth retreat), it would not have the same significance as an experience of what it means to be a part of the kingdom.

One of the most memorable experiences I had around Communion came a few years ago during a Maundy Thursday evening worship service. At this service right before Easter, the congregation where I served as youth pastor met to remember and celebrate Jesus' Last Supper before his crucifixion. Tables were set up in the sanctuary so we could all sit and serve one another the bread and the juice at the same time. (We're United Methodists, so it was grape juice.)

My table was one of the first ones to finish, and as I watched the others in the congregation serve one another, I was especially drawn to a table where a family of five—two adults and three children all under eight years old—was seated with an older couple and the senior pastor. One by one they passed the elements, hearing one say, "This is the body and blood of Christ," and saying the same to the next person in the circle. By this time, the cup and bread were coming around the table to be served to the final person—the senior pastor. I watched an expression of true missional communion as the youngest boy, Blake, who was only four, took the bread, broke off a piece, and said to the pastor, "This is the body of Jesus." He took the cup, handed it to the pastor (as all of us held our breath hoping that the grape juice wouldn't be spilled on the sanctuary carpet), and spoke with a look of certain innocence, "This is the blood of Jesus."

How many times had I seen and experienced this ritual before? Yet this time a young child was opening the door into the kingdom of God for me and for the rest of the congregation, allowing me to sit next to Christ at the sacramental table. We are blessed when all come to the table together. Let's not turn away that blessing and that experience of the kingdom.

# CHAPTER 4
# RELATIONSHIPS BASED ON PRESENCE

*I wondered if we had forgotten how to be friends to those who are so painfully isolated. I wondered why every member of every congregation couldn't be an adult friend to an adolescent in his or her community. I wondered if the church realized the power and possibility of relationships for transformation, and the theological mandate for action that is demanded of us by the incarnation.*
— Andrew Root, *Revisiting Relational Youth Ministry*

April Diaz, the former leadership development director at Newsong Church, in Irvine, California, recalls the time her senior pastor told the staff that he expected them to spend at least 20 hours a week working with people (as opposed to sitting at a desk and planning or writing). At first April thought this would be impossible. She had too many responsibilities and a full schedule. Then, after working on it and tweaking her days a bit, she realized it was only impossible if she continued to try to work within the constraints of how she'd been working. Once she began practicing the importance of building and sustaining relationships with her church members, April recognized the impact—and the possibilities—of spending so much time with others.[24]

As youth ministers, we hear (and speak) about how important it is to build relationships with youth. In fact, that imperative may be in the youth ministry job description at your church. We must be careful, though, lest our church members start to think that the youth minister is the one individual who is responsible for building relationships with teenagers. Likewise, this shouldn't be the responsibility of only the youth ministry team or volunteers. Rather, relationship building with teenagers is the task of the entire congregation.

Think about it: if we hire a youth pastor for the purpose of relating to teenagers, then isn't that similar to parents paying someone to be their child's friend? The youth in your congregation have God-given gifts that will be blessings for the growth and development of the rest of your church members, and, similarly, your congregation is the best group of people to relate to your teenagers. If you leave relationships up to the youth minister (and perhaps the youth ministry volunteers), then everyone will suffer and the ministry won't be sustaining. "Whatever kids you reach as a result of hiring a youth pastor will almost certainly stop attending after high school or when the youth pastor leaves."[25]

The mountain that has to be moved here is giving your congregation confidence in building those intentional, Christ-presence relationships. Adults who don't spend a lot of time with teenagers aren't sure that youth even want to get to know them. In fact, many adults are pretty convinced that most teens don't want to have anything to do with them.

Sometimes they're right. Sometimes a youth has had such negative (or even passive) relationships with adults that he or she is not interested in a relationship with anyone over 25. That's too bad—especially in the body of Christ, where we believe each person can be a living example of the presence of Christ.

My mother is a Christian educator. She's written books on raising children, on educating our young in the faith, and on being the presence of Christ in the community. She's taught countless workshops for churches and districts and entire regions at conferences in this country and abroad. I say all that to explain that she knows her stuff. Yet even someone who knows the congregation's duty to raise our children and youth can fall into this trap of uncertainty. One day, I was talking to her about the importance of the entire congregation being in individual, relational ministry with the youth, and Mom responded, "I guess I'm not very good at that. I sit next to a high school girl each week in choir rehearsal and on Sunday mornings in the choir loft, and I don't even know her name or where she goes to school." Mom just figured this teenage girl didn't want to know a lady in her 70s—someone who must have very little in common with her.[26]

With that attitude, why would we expect a youth to get involved in church ministries outside the youth group? Why would we expect a high school graduate to get involved in church ministries once they leave the youth group? It's no wonder 40 to 50 percent of our churched youth leave the church (and God?) once they graduate from high school. (This statistic is the impetus behind so much of what drives Kara Powell and Fuller Youth Institute's Sticky Faith research.) We've been teaching them (implicitly) that they have nothing in common with people over 25.

Some churches will ask only college students or young adults to be volunteers in their youth ministry, and they'll even hire youth staff only under the age of 35, believing anyone older cannot have any calling or ability to lead a youth ministry. I've heard senior pastors and search committees voice this belief, closing themselves off from experienced and capable youth ministers. It also teaches their youth and the congregation that there is no true connection between teenagers and the older part

67

of the body.

Andrew Root, author of *Revisiting Relational Youth Ministry*, says relational ministry "is an opportunity not to influence the influencers but to stand with and for those in need. True relational youth ministry shaped by the incarnation is a commitment to enter into the suffering of all, to offer all those in high school or junior high the solidarity of the church."[27] This kind of relationship involves much more than simply knowing a person's name or serving as a disciplinarian at youth gatherings. It means getting to know the other, being present with the other, and, most especially, it means being the Christ for the other. Root suggests that the reason relationships with youth are so difficult for adults is because these relationships are being approached as something people do, rather than something we enter into.

Beth Corrie is the director of the Youth Theological Initiative from Emory University. YTI gathers international youth who are interested in learning and talking about theology and meets with them for three weeks through the summer. (How's that for theology geeks?) Beth shares this story about the impact and opportunities for relationships:

> "Can you tell us a Bible story?" It was only the second night at the Youth Theological Initiative's three-week Summer Academy, and Anne, along with the four teenage girls living on her dormitory floor, were still getting to know each other. Anne had wandered into their suite shortly after the 11:00 pm dorm-check, sat down, and started to engage them in conversation.
>
> During this time before the midnight "lights-out," the youth can retire to their respective dorm rooms to unwind after a long day of activities and begin the process of getting ready for bed. Anne was entering her sixth

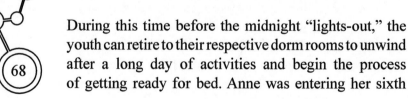

summer working for the Youth Theological Initiative (YTI), but was approaching this Summer Academy as her second time serving as an assistant director rather than a mentor. Having learned from her first summer as assistant director that the added responsibilities of supervising other mentors had detracted from her energy and time spent developing relationships with the "scholars" or youth participants, she had made a conscious commitment to get to know at least a few scholars well, even as she juggled her other tasks. With this in mind, she casually walked into the suite as the girls were gathered in one room talking, plopped down on the floor, and started the awkward process of getting to know a room full of strangers.

After chatting for several minutes, engaging in the typical "get-to-know-you" conversations, one of the girls asked Anne to tell them her favorite Bible story as a bedtime story. Anne had another idea. Sharing a favorite Bible story is a complicated task. So many stories are violent, disturbing, or include challenging messages about the cost of discipleship, particularly for first-world Christians. What the girls wanted was a bedtime story, something light-hearted and relaxing to help them settle down to sleep—Bible study was better saved for another time. So, Anne began instead to weave a tale on the spot about magical creatures coming to YTI and stumbling into awkward conversations and engaging in ridiculous icebreaker games. Silly and fanciful, the story struck the right note—she named the stresses they were all feeling about traveling alone from far away to a program full of individuals who, in many cases, dressed, talked, and thought differently from each other. She sent the signal, through gentle humor, that the awkwardness, homesickness, and disorientation was normal, and it was going to be OK. As the time

for lights out approached, the girls asked Anne if she would come back the next night for "story time."

Anne accepted their invitation, but decided before she returned the next night that she did not want to establish a dynamic in which she would be the fount of all stories, the charismatic leader surrounded by young people hanging on her words. She wanted the girls to be part of the process, to be active, not passive. When she sat down on the floor of the dorm room the next night, she explained to the girls that she didn't want to be the center of attention, and invited them to think about different ways they could do story time that would spread out the creativity—and responsibility. After some discussion, the group came up with the story time format they would follow for the remainder of the program: each night, a different person would be the storyteller, and the storyteller would narrate a tale in the "Mad-Libs" style, asking the person next to her in the circle to come up with a word to fill in the blank, thus sending the tale in a new direction that the storyteller would then need to build on and follow until she asked the next person in the circle to supply a key word for a blank. In this way, each person had a chance to be the storyteller, but the entire group helped to shape the story.

Anne continued to join the group for story time every night, but she was not in charge. She was an adult participating alongside youth.

Over the course of the three weeks, Anne noticed several dynamics developing, dynamics that became all the more obvious by comparison to what was taking place in suites that were not engaging in story time. First, in the minutes before story time commenced, Anne was able to engage in informal conversation that often yielded important insight into how the girls were relating to each other, and how the community as a whole was functioning. Sometimes she would walk into the suite and see that the girls were absorbed in a serious discussion. She would ask them what they were talking about, and sometimes they would look sheepishly at each other, trying to decide whether to tell her. Occasionally they would. More often, they would tell her that she would find out later, or that they would explain later. She didn't press it, but rather gave them permission to decide when and where to share their concerns. If she stayed and simply engaged in conversation, eventually they would share at least some of what was going on. By simply sticking around and being a part of the group, she was able to understand on a more complex level the social dynamics taking place throughout the community. But she had to listen; she had to be present without controlling the conversation.

Second, when story time ended and lights out was called at midnight, the girls in the storytelling suite turned off their lights and went to bed. They were "tucked in" and ready to end the day. In the other suites, staff members struggled to get the girls to turn off their lights, get into their own beds, and actually go to sleep. They had to ask numerous times and would frequently find scholars still up and talking long past midnight. In Anne's view, this was not because Anne was special, but simply because she had developed a level of trust and respect with the story time girls.

Third, by the final week, the story time girls no longer needed story time. After so many nights engaging in silly, informal conversation that served to create the space for building trust, the girls moved into deeper conversations with each other and with Anne,

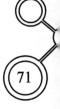

conversations in which they were able to become vulnerable, engage in self-critical reflection, and ask their most pressing questions about life, love and God.

As much as story time became a central ritual in the transition to bedtime for the girls in that room, there were other suites of girls in other parts of the dorm developing different patterns. By week two, the community had a "mean girl" problem, and much of it was being fed at night within the suites in which girls gathered but adults avoided.

Having sensed early on the value of this time in helping to develop trust with the girls who participated in story time, Anne had encouraged the other staff members to do something similar, to simply go up on the halls and hang out with the girls as they transitioned to going to bed. In the male dorm, the staff and scholars had developed a different pattern—a much smaller group overall, the entire dorm of scholars and staff spent their time between dorm-check and lights out hanging out together, playing games, instruments, and listening to music. In the girls' dorm, however, the pattern of going up to the rooms to hang out in cliques had developed early on, and it was clear that the staff members were not going to be able to entice the girls to change location and gather as one group. The adults needed to go where the girls were. The staff in the girls' dorm resisted this idea, however. From their perspective, the girls had spent the entire day in the presence of adults, and they felt strongly that the girls needed space and freedom. Going up and entering their suites to hang out felt like "surveillance." Citing the many ways in which young people today are indeed under the suspicious eye of institutions and adults, they saw giving the girls their space as a counter-cultural move. They didn't want to

be one more adult intruding and judging.

Yet, once a few of the staff members did go up on the floors to hang out, they realized that this was not surveillance. The girls wanted them there, and welcomed them into their space. It was true that they had had enough of adults standing on the edges of the room, watching and judging without participating, listening, or contributing to their discussions. It was true that they didn't want surveillance. It was not true, however, that they didn't want adults. They wanted adults—fully present, caring adults.[28]

In *Revisiting Relational Youth Ministry*, Andrew Root warns us (and we should warn our church members who enter into relationships with youth) not to settle for using relationships as a means to influence certain youth into doing "our thing" (even if "our thing" is an acceptance of Christ, becoming a participant in ministry, attending an event, or simply acting decent and disciplined). In fact, we have to be so very careful not to be in a results-motivated relationship that we must not allow youth to perceive an ulterior motive (because perception is what it's all about in relationships, regardless of our actual intent). In other words, if a youth perceives that the only reason you or one of the adults in your congregation is paying attention to him or her is to get him or her to come to a program or an event (or come to Christ), then the relationship (and the ministry and connection) is lost.

It is necessary for all who are in Christ-centered relationships to show that this relationship is for the long haul—through difficulties and through celebrations, when the youth is active in church and especially when he or she is not. That kind of commitment can be tough to communicate to an adult who already feels awkward connecting with someone 20, 30, or even 60 years younger. We want to see transformation,

but we forget that being the presence of Christ is already transformative. It's the miracle of the incarnation.

In many of my churches, I've set up a mentorship program for our confirmation students. During confirmation a young teen begins the journey of learning more about our faith and our church while at the same time engaging in some introspection to see where God has already been active in their faith journey so far. It's a great time to pair up a youth who is just entering into our ministry with an adult in the church. One such connection we made was between Daniel and Burt. Daniel was a seventh grader who was the epitome of an active and reckless middle school boy. He usually was a disturbance of some type in class, but he had a great sense of humor and came regularly to youth activities. Daniel didn't know any adults in the church, though, so he had no one to ask for as a confirmation mentor. I knew Daniel liked to play basketball, and with his sense of humor and his easygoing nature I thought Burt, a young adult who loved pickup basketball and seemed to relate well to middle school boys, would be a good mentor for him.

We tried to connect the two. We set up some times to meet. Daniel didn't show. Burt showed up at the door to class one day. Daniel said hi and was willing to stand for the introduction, but he quickly took off with friends. Burt called Daniel at his house, but Daniel was rarely at home (at least that was what Burt was told on the phone). And if he was home, Daniel spoke in monosyllabic answers and grunts. Burt tried inviting Daniel to meet him for ice cream or to sit with him in church. It never happened.

One day, after this had been going on for a frustrating two months, Burt suggested to me that perhaps he should just quit calling Daniel. "It's obvious that Daniel just doesn't want to have me as a mentor," Burt said with some disappointment.

I told him that was all the more reason that he should continue to be in touch—letting Daniel know he was praying for him daily (one of the duties of a confirmation mentor). It's possible that God will use such a connection so that one day Daniel recognizes the persistence of God's love and care for him—how God's love doesn't give up and doesn't depend on how Daniel responds. One day, with Burt giving this as an offering for God to use, Daniel may recognize that Christ has been knocking on his door through Burt and other church members.

The key, though, and the really hard part for Burt (and for all of us in a Christ-presence relationship) is that we may never get to experience or hear about Daniel being touched by what Burt did. Remember, the purpose behind these relationships cannot be in order to influence. Our calling is one of a companionship-oriented relationship and not one that is goal centered. As Dietrich Bonhoeffer teaches, we are in relationship because the Christ is in us—and he wants to be in relationship with those whom he loves. Through this kind of relationship—one that doesn't depend on a change or certain results and responses—we become the embodiment of Jesus Christ. We are vessels he uses to live out and suffer for the gospel. Each individual in your congregation can grow from this kind of incarnational/relational ministry. Experiencing Christ touching others through you is humbling and faith altering.

Jesus practiced this kind of relationship-based ministry. He met with the crowds, healing and speaking to them; from those crowds he called 72 and sent them out ahead of him to preach the gospel; of those he chose 12 disciples or apostles to be his closest companions; of those he had three who seemed to be his inner circle (Peter, John, and James, whom Jesus invited to the Transfiguration as well as to pray with him in the garden on the night he was betrayed). Finally, according to John, Jesus had one apostle with whom he was closer than the others.

As Andrew Root says, "Ministry is about connection, one to another, about sharing in suffering and joy, about persons meeting persons with no pretense or secret motives. It is about shared life, confessing Christ not outside the relationship but within it. This...is living the gospel."[29] But there is really no way to make adults get into relationships with teenagers. I don't have a sermon or program that will be an overnight success in motivating your congregation to build relationships with the young. There is no curriculum or study that will bring about immediate change in your church.

The best way to help the congregation change tracks and begin taking their relationships with youth more seriously, though, is to help them see that the heart of Christ (which is in them) is all about being with those he loves. If Christ loves teenagers, and if Christ is in us, then our hearts cannot help but be drawn to young people. If Christ welcomes children into his presence, then we all must. If the kingdom of God is entered only when we become like children, then in order to experience that kingdom we have to learn from the young as often as we can, participating in ministry and celebrations through their eyes and actions. Our task, as those who have answered the call to work with youth, is to help the rest of the congregation recognize this calling and to assure them that simply being present is a great place to start.

Chap Clark, coauthor of *Sticky Faith*, reminds us of the need for a ratio of five to one in youth ministry. That's a ratio I used to live by even 30 years ago when I first started planning youth events. I remember making many phone calls, trying to get one adult for every five youth going on a retreat or coming to a lock-in. Clark has called us all to task, though, and turned that ratio around. With our current understanding of the importance of relationships in ministry and the impact of a worshiping congregation on the lives of teenagers, Clark says that while the ratio is still five to one, it is now a recommended five adults for every one youth.[30]

Five adults for every one youth.

Think for a moment about one youth in your youth group. (Go ahead. Don't read any further until you've chosen a face or a name of one kid in your group.)

Now, stop that! Seriously, don't read any more until you've done it.

Got it? (If not, then keep thinking until you acknowledge who God is impressing upon you right now.)

I can wait.

OK. Write that name (or the person's initials) in the margin here or on a piece of paper. Now think of five adults in your congregation who are in some sort of positive relationship with that youth (other than the youth's parents). These significant individuals may be church staff, youth group volunteers, ushers, or the parent of a friend—five adult Christians who would greet that youth by name on a Sunday morning or at a chance encounter at a community basketball game. Write those five names under that youth's name.

Do it.

Is that an easy thing to do—to come up with five significant adults for one youth? Perhaps not. Maybe the youth you thought of is brand-new in your church. Maybe you thought of a real hard case—a kid who's nothing but trouble. And while there are at least 10 adults who know that youth by name, none of those are what you'd call "positive relationships." I'm convinced that the only way you and your church are going to sustain a connection with the person you named is when there

are at least five caring Christian adults looking out for that youth.

Look at the list again—even if you couldn't think of five adults. Are the adults only those who serve in the youth ministry? Or are there some from "outside the silo"? Your task—as the youth minister or as someone in your church who has a passion for helping connect the youth to your entire congregation—is to get every youth in your church connected to five significant adults who would walk across the room to greet that teenager. At least three of those should be adults from outside the youth room. If youth don't know how to be in relationship with adults involved in other ministries of the church, then they'll be lost when they are no longer in the youth ministry of the church as young adults. They will more easily become part of the 50 percent who check out of the church (and possibly from God) as they enter adulthood.

For many churches, this ratio goal isn't all that daunting. Most churches average under 100 people total (children, youth, and adults) in worship on a Sunday. The average-size youth group is only 12 to 15 youth. Those kinds of numbers are doable for connecting all of your youth. For some congregations, though, helping five adults connect with each of your youth is a full-time job. Remember what Andrew Root tells us about relationships—it's not something we do, but rather something we enter into.

Your task of helping adults be in relationship with the youth isn't one of finding activities and setting up mixers or mentorships. Your task is to point the adults to the Christ that is already living within them. Remind them of the vow they made (and continue to make each time a child is baptized or dedicated). Talk with adult classes and Bible studies; introduce youth when they approach you while you're talking to another adult; be an example of how an adult can welcome and relate to teenagers—but don't do it all yourself. A relationship takes time, and it's not something you can program or manipulate successfully.

# CHAPTER 5
# WHAT'S YOUR INTEGRATION FACTOR?

*The Integration Pastor will contribute to
and collaborate with the broader church for
meaningful, intentional, and mutual ways
to connect students to the Church.*
— Job description for the position of
youth integration pastor, Newsong Church

My father-in-law loved trains. He had the attic turned into "The Train Room" where he kept all of his O gauge trains. (Really, my wife says they couldn't call it an attic; it was The Train Room.) At Christmastime it became a tradition to put a small train around the Christmas tree in the living room. There were no gifts to be seen until Christmas morning, but the train and its village of antique houses and villagers were all around the tree for weeks before the special day.

I remember having to be careful just how fast the train was going on the track. Since it was so small—just enough track to make it around the tree—the curves were very tight. If the train built up too much speed on a straightaway, it would fly off the track at the next curve. This is true with real trains as well as automobiles. If you turn away too quickly from the direction you've been going, the vehicle will careen out of control and derail or fly off the track.

So how do we turn this fast-moving train known as your congregation in a different direction? Or, perhaps it's not so fast moving. Maybe your congregation makes changes very slowly. In either case, let's see how far the track needs to be moved and how to motivate your whole congregation into a more integrated understanding of what youth ministry is all about.

It's not advisable that you simply take new programs and start implementing them into your ministry. First of all, what we're talking about here isn't just a program; it's a way of thinking. And just trying to start some intergenerational activities won't get people moving very smoothly into the curve. The faith community needs to be on board with where you're trying to lead them. If you simply change direction without the necessary preparations, your train may fly off the tracks.

Try this: make photocopies of the questionnaire in this chapter, and hand it out to church leaders, Sunday school teachers, all of the staff, the various adult classes, Bible studies, small groups, and all of your youth group. Or you can post the questionnaire online and tally the results through *SurveyMonkey.com* or some other survey application.* Then, when you get your results, set up an hour to get together with everyone (or with each group you surveyed) and talk about the results. Go through the informative session (also found in this chapter) to begin casting the vision of what it means to be an integrated congregation. (If you're a large church, you may wish to start with just the staff or with just the leadership.)

It is important that you make the effort to share the survey results with your congregation. This time together will help introduce the topic of intergenerational and integrated ministries—why it's important, how it is God's call, how it's a part of our vow and role as Christians—and how your church lives up to this calling.

* Download an editable version of the survey at http://bit.ly/onebodysurvey

# AN INTERGENERATIONAL EVALUATION OF OUR CHURCH

Thank you for taking this survey. We'd like to find out how well we know each other in the congregation and the surrounding community. Please answer each question to the best of your knowledge. There are two age categories referred to in this survey: youth (age 12-18) or adult (age 18+). Whenever an "opposite age category" is mentioned, it is simply referring to whichever one is not your own.

First, we'd like a little background information:

1. Are you an adult (over 18) or a youth (age 12 to 18)? (Circle one)

2. How long have you been involved with this church?

3. Do you have family members of the same household who also go to this church? If so, are they adult, youth, or children?

4. Are you a student in college?

5. Do you have children in college?

6. If you have children, are any of them actively participating in the youth ministries of the church?

7. Including worship, how many ministries do you consider yourself involved in at our church?

**Please circle the letter next to the answer that best describes your response to these questions:**

1. Think of the last few times you went to a worship service at the church. How many people in the opposite age category (if you are an adult, then how many youth; if you are a youth, then how any adults) did you see in attendance at those times of worship? (Guessing is allowed.)

   a. There's usually only a very small number, if any at all.

   b. A few of the opposite age category were there—maybe 10 to 20 percent of the congregation, but no more than that.

   c. I was definitely in the minority—over half of the people there were of the opposite age group.

   d. A good representation—under half, but quite a crowd (20% to 50%).

   e. A good number were there—close to half of those worshiping in the room were of the opposite age category.

2. Think of people (other than family members) that you know in the opposite age category *by name*. How many would you intentionally walk up to and call by name if you saw them?

   a. 0-1

   b. 2-3

   c. 4-5

d. 6-7

e. 8+

3. Not counting a designated Youth Sunday, on how many different Sundays did at least one youth help lead some part of the main worship service in the last four months (singing, playing music, ushering, reading Scripture, preaching, announcements, drama, etc.)?

   a. 0

   b. 1

   c. 2-5

   d. 6-9

   e. 10+

4. In how many different leadership roles have you seen a youth participating in the main worship service in the last six months (singer, musician, usher, greeter, Scripture reader, preacher, sound technician, video technician)?

   a. None in the last six months

   b. One or two of these in the last six months

   c. Three or four

   d. At least once a month a youth does one of these in worship

   e. Almost weekly a youth is serving in some way in worship

5. Does the church have a separate youth worship service?

   a. I don't know.

   b. Yes, at the same time as the main service.

   c. Yes, but not every week. At least once a month they're asked to attend the main worship service.

   d. Yes, but on a different day/time than the main worship service.

   e. No. Youth and adults are expected to attend the same worship service.

6. Do youth serve on any of your church committees?

   a. No. Youth don't even plan their own ministries.

   b. No. Youth serve only on youth ministry planning teams.

   c. I don't know.

   d. Yes. Youth serve on one or two committees or teams besides youth leadership teams.

   e. Yes. We try to have a youth serve on every team or committee.

7. Have you prayed for someone from our church in the opposite age category by name (other than a family member) in the last six months?

   a. I don't know anyone in that category at my church (other than family).

   b. I haven't.

c. I have, only because they were on the prayer list or mentioned in worship.

d. I have many times (or I'm in a class/group that does regularly).

e. Yes, almost daily I pray for this person (or these people).

8. Have you ever spoken at or attended a class, Bible study, or small group or ministry mostly made up of people from outside your age category (if you are a youth, then a children's or adult group; if you are an adult, then a youth or a children's group) in the last year?

   a. I don't know about groups outside my own age category.

   b. No. I know of some groups, but I don't see any need to go or I don't feel welcome to attend those groups.

   c. No, but I would like to sometime soon.

   d. Yes, but it's not something I'm likely to do again.

   e. Yes, and I met some folks who made me feel very welcome there.

9. Could you name someone from the opposite age category (not a family member and not a church staff member) through whom you felt the presence of Christ or who brought you closer to the kingdom of God?

   a. No. I can't see anyone of the opposite age

category ever fulfilling that role for me.

b. No. I'm just not in that kind of relationship or understanding with anyone in the opposite age category.

c. No. I used to a long time ago, but one of us grew up or moved away.

d. Yes, and I can see how one or both of us have grown stronger in faith because of it.

e. Yes, more than one fits this type of relationship from the opposite age category.

10. If asked by the pastor or a youth leader, how likely are you to share a short account of your story with at least one person from the opposite age category?

a. Not likely at all. I don't feel comfortable talking about myself.

b. I'd probably do this if no one else steps up, but I wouldn't enjoy it.

c. I'd be willing, although it's not something I would seek out.

d. I would appreciate someone showing me where my story would be helpful.

e. I'm very willing to do this, and I have done it already on at least one occasion.

For scoring, give yourself one point for each "a" answer, two points for each "b," and so on. With 10 questions, scores will range from 10 to 50 points.

Now tally the points from the survey. The highest score possible is 50 points. (Doubled would give you a score for your church based on 100, allowing you to grade your church's integration factor on an A, B, C, D, or F scale.) You should also categorize the answers by who answered—youth or adults, college students, parents. Remember, this score reflects the perception (realized or unrealized) of your congregation toward its own integration. The significance of this is that it can also reflect on how your congregation lives out the gospel as an inclusive and present body of Christ.

Next, set up a time to host the following session where you can present the survey results as well as begin casting this vision of a greater integration of youth into the whole life of your congregation. (Note: It would also be good to make this session available online as a PowerPoint presentation.)

# A TIME TO REFLECT AND DREAM: A SESSION FOR THE YOUTH AND ADULTS IN YOUR CHURCH

## Consider

It would be good to have the date and time and location of this informative session printed on the survey so those who answer the questions will be able to make plans to attend. Make this time together one of integration, since that's the point of the whole survey. Invite the youth, their parents, and other adults in the congregation. Some of the activities here work best when there are multiple generations present from within the church to participate. Advertise that any are welcome; participants don't need to have completed a survey to attend.

## Prior to This Session

Do some statistical research regarding your congregation.

- First, gather a list of all youth (members and nonmembers) who are on your rolls from the past year. This should include even those who've declared your church as their church home but might not attend often (or at all).

- Find out how many of those have been coming to youth ministry activities in the last six months (or as far back as you might be able to go—even if it's only a few weeks).

- Also figure out the percentage of youth who attend the main worship services. If you have a separate youth worship service, then get that percentage too. (It helps to do this as percentages of your total number, rather than simply a number. A percentage puts it up against the potential.)

- Finally, find out how many youth are involved in or have visited church ministries outside the youth ministry (such as nursery, choir, an adult Bible study or class, church suppers, ushering).

## You Will Need:

- Newsprint or a whiteboard and markers

- Bibles

- Survey results posted on newsprint or on PowerPoint slides

- Statistics printed on paper for display around the room (separate from the survey results)

- Names of all the youth on your church roles (active and inactive) printed on 3x5 cards—one per card (no addresses or contact information)

- Masking tape

- Blank 3x5 cards or nametags for each participant

- Pencils or pens for each participant

## Preparation

- Have the results of the survey either posted on separate newsprint pages or on separate slides (one question and its result per page).

- Go through some of the suggested ministries and practices in chapter 7 of this book. Be prepared to use a few of these as examples of ways to keep your age-level ministries while still promoting integration of the whole congregation. Understand that people may at first hear you suggesting that youth ministries be abandoned and replaced by integration. Part of the purpose of this session is to help people understand that there are many creative ways to integrate and collaborate while still keeping age-level ministries intact.

- Place masking tape on the backs of each 3x5 card with the name of a youth written on each card. Stick the cards to either an empty wall, a table top, or on the back of each empty chair in the room. (Meeting in the sanctuary adds another visual dynamic of each of these names being a part of our worshiping community.)

- Have these instructions printed on a whiteboard or poster for all to see as they enter the room:

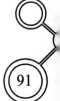

Welcome! It's good that you have come to this gathering. We are all among a group of caring people who want to understand a little more about ourselves and what God is trying to do with us in ministry to the world. We'll begin in just a few minutes. But in the meantime, please take a blank card and write your name in the center of it and the name of someone who's been significant to your faith in the lower right-hand corner. This person may or may not be someone in our church. Then wear that nametag for the first part of our time together.

- Hang some posters with the following statistics printed on them around the room on the walls, bulletin boards, or chairs: (Note: this will require some preparation ahead of time to find out the percentages that apply to your church so you can replace the XXs with your current statistics.)

  - 40% to 50% of high school seniors who have come to the church will drop away from the church and from God for at least one year after high school.

  - XX% of the youth we have on roll have come to a youth ministry activity or program at least once in the last year.

  - XX% of the youth we have on roll have come to the main worship service in the past year.

  - The parent is the most influential individual in the faith development of most teenagers.

  - XX% of our youth at this church are involved in a ministry outside the youth ministries of the church.

# Do This

- Begin by greeting people and pointing out the nametag instructions on the poster or board. (Make sure you also wear a nametag.) Let the participants move around the room and look at some of the posters with the statistics. Feel free to talk about some of the stats or answer questions as you wait for everyone to arrive.

- Ask everyone to be seated and begin with a prayer, asking God to help your congregation be connected and together in ministry. Be thankful for the individual gifts that we all have, too, and the ways those gifts help lift each other up and strengthen the body of Christ.

- On newsprint (or a whiteboard) write the word *intergenerational*. Ask, "What does this word mean in the context of a church?" Write any responses under the word. Ask, "What are the differences between intergenerational ministry and multigenerational ministry?" After a few answers, explain that multigenerational is ministry that is available to people of different ages but doesn't necessarily mean those different ages interact. Intergenerational ministries involve people of different ages, and those involved work together in ministry, drawing on one another's gifts and talents and building up the community by working together. (Note: An example of the difference might be seen in a church supper. When all are invited to and attend the supper, it can be called multigenerational. Each age group might ignore the other ones and sit at their own table, never recognizing the other generations at the function. However, if different age groups mix at tables and interact with each other, then they begin to experience something intergenerational.)

- Tell the group you hope this meeting will be intergenerational. Then ask about the benefits we might find or experience in intergenerational ministries. Talk about these benefits and blessings for a few minutes. Ask, "Why might we feel hesitant about intergenerational ministries? Why might some hesitate in becoming more integrated in our congregation?" Explain that you hope to show the importance of integrating the youth (and children) into the life of the whole church, and assure people that there are ways to do this without losing age-level ministries like youth ministry or adult classes.

- Introduce the survey, reminding those who took the survey of the way it was scored and who was polled. (Remember that some may be present who did not take the survey.)

- Show each survey question to the group, then give the results for each question. Help participants understand that this survey reflects how the congregation is per-ceived. Some answers might not portray the true situation, but the responses are what we use to determine the integration score for the congregation and its ministries. (The survey answers may show that few or no youth are seen in worship when, in reality, manyyouth may be present in worship but no one realizes they are there.) Provide time to reflect on or to respond to each question.

- After you have shown the whole survey and the results, reveal the score for your church. Ask if there were any results that were surprising. Point out some misguided perceptions (if any), and answer any questions people may have about the youth ministries and the congregation.

- Ask participants to find someone in the room they don't know that well, if possible (or it could be simply some one they did not come to the meeting with), and tell him or her about the person whose name they wrote on their nametag (the one who influenced them in their faith). Ask them to explain how knowing that person helped their faith grow stronger. Then ask, "How can some of those traits or practices that positively influenced us help us now as we relate to each other in our church?"

- If your church has a vow that it takes upon the dedication or baptism of children, share that vow now. Then ask, "Why might we as Christians individually and corporately be responsible for building relationships with our children and youth?" (If your church does not have a specific vow, then simply ask the above question.) Explain that no Christian is exempt from the call to be in ministry with our young.

- Take about 10 minutes to go through some of the questions from the survey again, and this time ask what kinds of things your church could do that might help the setting described in that question be more integrated or intergenerational. Especially look at any questions that may have had surprising responses.

- Use a few examples that you have marked from chapter 7 of this book as examples of ways to build integration among your congregation. Help the participants recognize that the goal of this focus is to help sustain the faith of our youth after they have left high school and moved into adulthood. Use the statistic of about 40 to 50 percent of youth leaving the church as a caution against being too divided in ministry and a warning of the need to be more integrated.

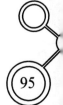

- Direct everyone's attention to the nametags that are posted with all of the youth names. Ask the adults in the room to count how many of the names they can at least put a face with. Explain Dr. Chap Clark's teaching that we should have a ratio of five adults who would seek out and connect with every one youth in our church (see chapter 4). Ask if this is a realistic goal for your church.

- If youth are present, ask them to take their own nametags from the ones displayed. Next, ask adults to take away any nametags of the youth they know and would recognize in a worship service. Finally, point out that the remaining names represent those teenagers who are unknown by the adults in this room. Ask for feedback. If little or none is given, point out how workable Dr. Clark's vision is for your congregation—to connect five adults in a caring, watchful relationship with each teenager. If there are many, many youth names left over, point out that these are just youth who are not known in this group. Ask how you might all, as a congregation, begin working toward the goal of five adults to every single youth.

- Ask for any comments or concerns. If there are people who'd like to help with this new direction for your congregation, invite them to form a sort of "integration task force" that will come up with creative ways to communicate this need to the whole congregation.

- Close with a prayer. Suggest that each adult take at least one name and pray for that person daily for the next month, asking God to help that youth connect with the congregation in a meaningful way and to show that adult ways he or she might connect with this youth and others.

It is vital that you continue to share about this topic after the initial meeting, either through a task force or the staff. You may need to offer a few extra meeting times in order to repeat this session with a strong number of church members. Once you've communicated where the church is going with this, they will understand why various ministries are trying an intergenerational approach and hopefully not be afraid of this new focus.

# CHAPTER 6
# STUMBLING BLOCKS AND PITFALLS

*When opportunity knocks the wise will build bridges
while the timorous will build dams. It is a new day.*
—Lamin O. Sanneh

I hesitate to write a chapter full of pitfalls and barricades that exist in our churches. Some practices and traditions have happened for perfectly understandable reasons; some habits and programs are deeply ingrained and will take quite a while to change. ("We've always done it this way. It brings in the numbers, so it must be successful.") As someone who is often called by churches to consult on ways of doing youth ministry, I don't want to flippantly say, "You shouldn't do things this way." Every context has its needs and its reasons for what may seem appropriate or necessary.

It is good to recognize, though, how some of our most common youth ministry practices can also work against integrating our youth into the life of the church. If we're going to adopt a certain practice, then we must also be sure to understand how some of those practices or traditions might strengthen the silos and push us away from integration. Like much in ministry, the presence of some of these situations isn't necessarily all bad or all good. When you recognize any of these practices that have potential of disrupting a true experience of the kingdom in your ministry, weigh the positives and negatives against

what may happen if you try to make changes. Then evaluate what it will take to overcome the walls blocking integration. While practices mentioned in this chapter might be present and currently unchangeable in your church, the examples will give you some insight for future goals or how to compensate in other areas.

As you read through these hindrances to integration, note which ones are present in your church. Perhaps there is a current discussion going on around that specific topic. Make sure the leaders who are a part of the decision-making process understand all of the dynamics around the choice being made.

---

Our youth minister asked the youth for permission to cancel youth group one Sunday night so the whole church could gather for a special dinner that was to focus on a new building campaign. The church was small, and they needed the fellowship hall and kitchen for this meal—spaces that we also needed and used every Sunday night. We were on board with this, and we agreed to give up our youth space for one night since we were also invited to attend the dinner and celebrate and plan with the whole congregation. It was a great opportunity for the whole church to move together on this new area of growth.

On the night of the dinner, more people showed up than were expected, and the leadership of the church realized that some people would need to sit in the Sunday school rooms down the hall—away from the rest of the gathering. We youth were pretty upset when we were asked to move down the hall to eat separately. It felt like we were being pushed to the kids' table. It took a long time for us to participate with the whole congregation in anything else.

— Shannon

Think about how difficult it might be to change course, and make note of some possible ways to "slow down the train" or use other practices to compensate for the limitations of another. Continue to be mindful of these areas as your ministry progresses. It's possible that a season of change or transition will arise, at which time you and your youth ministry team could introduce ideas for moving toward youth integration.

## Stumbling Block 1: Dividing Youth (and Children) from Corporate Worship

Offering a separate youth worship service has become a popular and effective program for many youth ministries. Rather than blending a short worship time into a night of fun and games, an intentional hour or so of worship for youth allows those who are interested in worship to participate in something they know will remain focused—avoiding the bait-and-switch of a night mixing games and worship. It also means those youth who are coming for just games or socializing will know this is not the time or place for that. Youth worship can be powerful and can feature specifically the kinds of music that youth enjoy; it can focus its prayers on the needs of those in the youth community; it builds unity in the youth participants.

Some churches provide this youth worship time at a separate time from the main worship services. Others schedule it at the same time as the "adult" worship services, allowing a choice for youth to either worship with the whole congregation (and their families) or split off and worship on their own. Oftentimes the children have their own worship service too, meaning that the main service is mostly an adult service. Usually this happens in larger churches (often for reasons of space, reducing the distraction of children, or offering youth a different style of worship). But smaller congregations have chosen this type of schedule too, as they've seen how it keeps youth engaged and active on Sunday mornings in larger churches and feel compelled to compete with their programming.

The risk of offering a youth worship service (or any youth program, for that matter) during the main worship time is that youth are tempted (and often encouraged) to gather or worship apart from the rest of the congregation. This separates youth from their families (biological as well as faith family). Some would say this isn't so bad. If it brings in more youth to worship, then why not? If youth aren't being reached in the main worship time, then why not give them a worship service that is focused more on youth and the issues they face?

This is the argument I heard as I consulted with a small country church with less than 100 in the main worship service. The youth minister wanted to start a youth worship service in order to get the five to ten older youth to come to Sunday morning worship. When I told her she and the congregation may be losing out on helping the youth feel like a part of the whole congregation, she pointed out that these older youth weren't coming at all now. "At least with this youth worship service, they will start to participate in worship regularly."

It takes a lot of time and energy to start and carry off a separate worship service for youth—whether you have 10 or 100 show up. What if one spent a bit of that same energy trying to come up with ways to make the main worship service significant for people of all ages before tossing the children and youth out to their tribal spaces? The community of worshipers could look for ways to help engage those 10 youth into a care system that not only helps them get to church for worship, but also plugs them in to the service in ways that engage them with the community.

When we take youth and children out of worship, we cut off the whole congregation from an effective witness to all ages. Youth no longer see their neighbors and parents in worship.

Children no longer learn what it means to worship as an integrated community. Adults cannot experience the presence of the young in worship and the way those young continue to point them to God's kingdom. The biblical model of raising children in the faith and including them in acts of community worship is ignored in order to get a fast boost to numbers. Once youth are too old for youth ministry, they must start worshiping with a community they don't know (and one that doesn't know them).

Too often I have spoken with those who used to be very active in my church's youth ministry, but as adults they find themselves frustrated because they "can't find a church like I experienced in youth group." Without an intergenerational worship experience, young adults enter into corporate worship unable to feel a part of the community.

If your church is in this situation (where it offers a youth worship service at the same time as the main service), there are a few things you can do:

1.  you can work to change the program right away—dropping the youth worship and encouraging youth to join the rest of the community together in worship;

2.  you can move the youth worship to another day or time so the youth can still have their own worship but also can be in worship with the community; or

3.  you can keep things the way they are but work extra hard in other ways to compensate for the walls that are being built.

Changing the program right away is sometimes helpful, as it will awaken your youth and the rest of your congregation to the importance and calling of worshiping in a combined

community of faith. However, this kind of change might be too fast, and it should only be carried out with clear communication regarding the vision and purpose of worship. The leadership should be informed and educated on the scriptural and practical reasons; the youth should be brought in on the purpose; and parents should be introduced to the "why" before it actually happens. Help the congregation understand that this is a move toward sustaining the faith of your youth beyond their high school years.

Moving youth worship to another day or time can also be a strong option. Giving the youth their own time, place, and expression of worship is key to their faith development. This still allows families to worship together at the main service. However, if youth begin attending only the youth worship service, then their lack of integration into the worshiping community will need to be bolstered in other ways.

It may be too soon to switch back to a community-wide worship, and you may decide that keeping worship divided and running concurrently with the main worship is necessary for the near future. Mike Park, student integration pastor at Newsong Church in Irvine, California, tried an immediate change back to corporate worship. But after receiving much pushback and what seemed like strong negative reaction, they changed back to having youth worship at the same time for three out of four Sundays. On the fourth Sunday of each month, the entire congregation is encouraged to worship together. We do this in my own church, but the youth have started using that fourth Sunday as a reason to stay home from worship.

If you choose to keep the concurrent youth and main worship scheduling (or are considering it), then make sure you still communicate with your church leadership about the possible hazards and shortfalls of this model. Remind the leadership again and again in the worship committee and the church council meetings that keeping youth divided during worship only strengthens the silo mind-set. It may be that the church leaders will revisit the option of change in the future. It is also important that the whole leadership recognize the efforts you and other youth leaders will take toward integrating the youth—ways that will try to compensate for anything the youth may lose in having divided worship.

## Stumbling Block 2: Having a Separate Youth Building or Youth Wing

When a church gives the youth some space for its ministry, it is usually a sign of support and not an intent to put the youth out of sight and out of the way. If the youth ministry isn't careful, though, a separate wing, building, or even youth room can become a youth silo—something divided from the rest of the community and separate from the body of Christ.

The benefits of a separate space for the youth are many. It shows support of the youth. It communicates to those inside the church, as well as in the outlying community, that the congregation values youth ministry. Having their own place gives teenagers a space that can easily be furnished and decorated on a more permanent basis for the learning and socialization needs of youth. They have more room for their kinds of games and their models of small groups and worship. There is nothing more frustrating for a youth leader than trying to lead a Bible study or have a youth group time in a room that is set up for preschool—stocked with small tables, miniature chairs, cartoon characters painted on the wall, and its own play kitchen. (Really, I've taught youth Bible studies in these situations before. It's frustrating and confining.) Youth need assurance that their presence is known and appreciated.

The possible problem of a separate youth ministry space, however, is akin to a son whose bedroom is outfitted with everything he needs—a refrigerator, a television, comfortable

furniture, a computer, perhaps even his own bathroom. With a setup like this, it's a wonder his family would see him much at all. My own son who is a high school senior has a similar setup, and we see him when he comes out for food, to shower, and when we need his dirty dishes.

While autonomy is important for an adolescent, relationships with the rest of the faith family are also crucial for the teenager and the other generations in the faith community. Creating a sanctum in the youth wing will possibly nurture the teenager through the high school years, but that isn't very sustainable, and it doesn't help those youth learn what it means to be a part of the whole body of Christ. By the time they graduate from high school, they will have a hard time connecting with the church as a whole and may find themselves looking for a church that is a youth ministry for young adults (starting the cycle all over again).

While I would never recommend getting rid of a designated youth ministry space, it is important to exercise practices that help keep this space from strengthening the silo. One way to overcome the possible hazards of having a divided youth space is to bring adults into that space on a regular basis—adults who are not the regular youth ministry volunteers. Invite Mr. Davis in to tell about his experiences overseas; bring in the head usher or the choir president to explain why they enjoy their particular ministry; ask Mrs. Jenkins to tell her story of being adopted (and link it with our Christian adoption and being children of God). Always be on the lookout for ways to strengthen ties to the rest of the congregation and help youth feel comfortable with those beyond the walls of the youth building.

It is helpful to plan a youth space central to the rest of the church and not someplace across the parking lot or down in the last wing of the education building. I remember Dr.

Don Saliers, professor emeritus of theology and worship at Candler School of Theology, explaining to a committee of lay leaders how their proposed design for a new worship space communicated the congregation's priorities and understanding of its mission in the community. He spoke of how a prominent main doorway facing the front of the property spoke to people about how open the church is to the community and how the placing of classrooms or the position of the pews in the sanctuary communicated different understandings of education and the worshiping community. Imagine what kinds of priorities and values would be communicated to the congregation, the youth, and anyone who enters the space if the youth and children's areas are central to the rest of the church. How might we model an "embracing of our youth" through the architecture and layout of our church?

Hillside UMC, in Woodstock, Georgia, has a very large youth ministry. And at one time the youth wing was upstairs at the end of a back hallway. No one needed to venture into those halls and rooms if they were unassociated with the youth ministry. Through the years and because of some structural and practical needs, the youth space has now moved to the entrance of the educational area of the church. It's at a main entrance, and many in the congregation walk right through the youth gathering area each Sunday when they come to church. What a great way to bring the congregation together. Sure, at times there may be a disruption, but with some care and foresight the benefits of what's communicated far outweigh the few drawbacks of having the youth out front.

## Stumbling Block 3: Hiring Someone to "Be in Relationship" with Your Youth

It's not uncommon for me to sit with a group of pastors talking about their needs for youth ministry, and when I ask them what they look for in a youth minister, the first answer is, "Someone who can relate well to teenagers."

Obviously relating to teens and having a love for teenagers are essential in an effective youth minister, but are these the most important characteristics? Many youth ministry job descriptions include the phrase, "someone who can relate to teenagers." In fact, many churches (and senior pastors) even put an age restriction on this description, certain that the youth minister must be under 40 years of age in order to be significant in the lives of youth. (See the next stumbling block.) When the congregation has this mind-set—relying on youth ministers to be the only ones to reach and relate with the youth—then the result can be the congregation simply forgets about its responsibility to raise youth in the faith. They have sold out that calling and responsibility to whomever they hired to do the job.

Recall the quote printed in chapter 4 from Mark Riddle's book, *Inside the Mind of Youth Pastors*—"Whatever kids you reach as a result of hiring a youth pastor will almost certainly stop attending after high school or when the youth pastor leaves."[31] I would turn that around a little and say, "If a youth is connected to the church only because of a relationship with the youth pastor or the volunteers, then he or she will almost certainly stop attending after growing out of the youth ministry (or once that significant adult leaves)."

If your church has the mind-set that only the youth pastor and youth ministry volunteers have the job of relating to the youth, then help the entire congregation see that this is a calling and expectation for everyone. In the United Methodist Church we have a vow that we take at a child's baptism or at confirmation:

> With God's help, we will so order our lives after the example of Christ, that this child, surrounded by steadfast love, will be established in the faith and confirmed and strengthened in the way that leads to life eternal.[32]

Perhaps your church takes a similar vow at the dedication or recognition of children or youth. Notice that we do not promise to hire someone to strengthen the faith of this child or to find a few volunteers to take this charge. We vow to order our lives in such a way that Christ will be experienced by this child through each of us. That's a huge commitment, and it can only be fully realized when each person in the congregation reaches out to the youth in the community.

## Stumbling Block 4: Using Only College Students or Young Adults as Volunteers

We understandably gravitate toward the younger church members when looking for youth ministry leaders. If we want someone who will fully participate, then it often takes someone with a little less metal—less silver in their hair, less gold in their teeth, and less lead in their...behinds—to get out on the floor, into the field, or into the swimming pool to play with the youth. A youthful energy is required for lock-ins, pool parties, capture the flag, and dodgeball. But there is more to youth ministry than games and lock-ins, and there are more in the body of Christ than people under 30 years of age.

Limiting those involved in youth ministry to only college students or young adults limits the outreach, the connections, and the potential of your youth ministry. It feeds into the separation of the youth from the rest of the congregation and closes off some of your most able adults from enjoying connections with youth and experiencing the kingdom through teenagers.

When I first began serving as a youth minister at a church near Canton, Georgia, I was invited to have lunch with the older adult group that met monthly in the fellowship hall. I sat at a table next to a lady in her mid-80s named Ruth. As we talked about youth ministry, she spoke of the fun she had as a youth in church and even as an adult leader when she was younger

(more than 50 years ago). Ruth said she regretted that she was too old to work with the youth anymore. I assured her I would love to have someone in her 80s or even 90s spending time with the youth. I told her she had stories, insight, and understandings no other adult leaders could contribute to our youth. I had a small group of girls in mind that would be blessed by her presence, and I invited her to prayerfully consider partnering with another leader for this small group.

After a few weeks, Ruth called and said she would love to be a part of the small group.

Unfortunately, the girls wanted nothing to do with Ruth. They wouldn't give her a chance. They were sure an older lady would find no connection with them, and they were afraid that opening up to Ruth would feel like sharing personal things with their grandmothers—not something they regularly did or imagined.

I continue to mourn this opportunity that was lost. Ruth was an open, vivacious Christian lady. Had I not been so new, and had the partnering adult been on board with my choice, I might have held firmly with placing Ruth in the group. I let it go, though, and shortly thereafter, Ruth discovered she had cancer. Her resolve was to put her health in God's hands and decline painful and difficult therapy, believing she'd already had a fruitful and blessed life and was too old to struggle with the surgery and radiation. It would have been powerful to see her relationship with those five girls as they experienced the faith process and grieved together. Many church members were touched by Ruth's witness during those last months of her life, but the girls in that small group were not.

We could blame the girls for their reluctance, but they were only acting on what they'd already learned or perceived. Somewhere along the way these teenagers had decided that older, gray-haired adults could have no meaningful relationship with or influence on them. They missed out on experiencing Ruth's grasp of the kingdom and her exultation as it drew nearer.

## Stumbling Block 5: Limiting the Volunteer Pool to Parents of Your Youth

It's natural for a church to turn to the parents of teenagers for help in the youth ministry. After all, many parents offer to help as drivers, chaperones, or hosts, and some consider opening their homes or basements as a ministry opportunity. Some churches have no problem finding adult volunteers simply because the parents step up and do what's needed.

Take care not to let your parents dominate the volunteer base or leadership in your youth ministry. While I wouldn't suggest turning your back on a parent helper, it is essential that the volunteer base in a youth ministry be as diverse as the congregation—comprised of people of both genders as well as various life stages, ages, vocations, skills, and experiences. Just as your ministry would be limited by having all college-age volunteers, an all-parent leadership would cut off individuals who are called to meet the needs of the youth in your church.

Find ways to help adults in all stages of life know they have a calling to meet the faith needs of your youth. Also ask the parents of your teenagers to bring in other adults as they look for ways to strengthen the faith of their children. As you invite adults in to share their stories or as you connect mentoring adults with individual teens, you'll be able to view how they interact with teenagers. You will find insight into the personal faith journeys of adults in your church through various ministries. Use these insights and prayer to come up with your "discipleship dream team" of people who will guide your youth to the ministry and care of the whole congregation.

## Stumbling Block 6: Confirming or Dedicating Your Youth at a Separate Service from the Rest of the Church

Some churches have a confirmation class or new member class for youth who, at a specific date on the church calendar, profess a commitment to Christ and officially join the church. Often this is done during a normal worship service in front of the whole congregation, which follows the traditions of the church through millennia. In some communities, though, churches schedule a time on a Saturday or Sunday night (or on a youth retreat) for a special ceremony solely focused on bringing new youth members into the life of the church. How ironic when the very ceremony that recognizes youth as part of the congregation of believers and welcomes them into the body of Christ is held a separate time, divided from the congregation.

I understand the dynamics around this choice. The rationale at the church I currently attend is that there simply isn't space in the Sunday morning worship service for the many youth, family members, and friends who want to be a part of the celebration. We also like to design the service totally around the confirmation experience, and we don't feel as welcome to do that in the main worship time.

But what are we communicating to the youth, to their families, and to the rest of the congregation when we don't celebrate these new members and their decision to accept Christ in front of the entire faith community? What better time could there be to introduce them to the congregation? If your church has more than one main worship service, invite the youth to either come to all of the services that day or just the one their family usually attends. Another option is to take the service outside—or to another location where everyone can fit in the worship space. Though it's not the same as meeting in your own worship space, it will create new memories of a time when the entire church got together to celebrate its growth.

If a separate confirmation service cannot be avoided—maybe it's been happening this way for too long or there just isn't room for everyone to attend together—then make sure you take pictures and show them during worship the following Sunday. Invite one or two of the students to speak in the main Sunday worship about their decision and faith experiences in your church. Bring the youth who were just confirmed to the front of the sanctuary so they can be recognized and the congregation can meet and greet them at the end of the service. Do whatever you can to counteract the message that these new members are being kept separate from the rest of the body. Invite the whole congregation into the celebration.

## Stumbling Block 7: Allowing Your Youth Minister/ Staff Person to Focus Only on Youth and Their Families

While I served as the associate pastor at a church in Ohio for a number of years, I had many roles—including youth ministry. My hope was to one day convince the church to change my role into solely that of youth minister and hire another associate pastor to fulfill the duties I felt were outside the realm of youth ministry. I got frustrated when the senior pastor would assign me to hospital visitations, women's luncheons, or funerals with people who had no ties to our youth. These expectations seemed to take up the time I wanted to spend focusing on and growing the youth ministry. I enjoyed being a part of the worship planning, but doing that and attending staff meetings took up much of my weekly schedule. How could I promote and develop youth ministry if I had to work in all of these other areas as well?

Years after those meetings and visits and funerals and luncheons, I discovered that all that time I'd been planting seeds of support and connection in my congregation for youth ministry. When people saw me at those events, they knew me as the youth minister—even if my visit with them was about something else. They often asked questions about what the youth were doing, about what we did on our various trips, and about how they could best support the young people. They wanted to hear stories of the youth in their faith community. As I got to know more about adults in the congregation, I found it easier to connect their stories with the individual teenagers in my care. When I got to know Mr. McCoy, it was natural to connect him with Jeremy or Tyler—two students who also loved music and played the trumpet. When Justin needed a mentor, I knew Mr. Johnson was just the person to ask. When we needed someone to host an outing or stand in for a sick Sunday school teacher, I knew whom to call.

*If we expect our youth to be a part of the whole congregation and not just the youth group, then we must lead the way as youth ministers in getting to know the whole congregation.*

One of the best hospital visits I had was with an older gentleman (with no connection to the youth ministry) who'd had an accident while cutting down trees. He was alone when it happened, and after his accident, despite severe internal injuries, he had to pull himself off the jutting tree limb (you don't want to know where it was stuck) and crawl up a hill to his car and cell phone. As I listened to him talk about his prayer during his struggle and how he felt God's connection with him during that experience, I realized that the middle school Sunday school class needed to hear this guy speak. I invited him to come tell his story a few weeks after his recovery and share how his faith gave him strength and encouragement in his struggle. That class went so well, the man immediately asked if he could teach the class every Sunday. Years later he still was an effective and caring teacher of middle schoolers. (And it helped that he could describe his experience with all the gore and drama that middle school boys and girls find interesting.)

If we expect our youth to be a part of the whole congregation and not just the youth group, then we must lead the way as youth ministers in getting to know the whole congregation. If we expect the congregation to reach out and invite the youth into its leadership and ministries, then we must introduce them to the youth on personal levels. Don't allow the youth minister (especially if it's you!) to stay in the silo. The very responsibilities I tried to get out of are ones I now believe all youth ministers should have: visiting the sick, speaking at luncheons, and helping with Vacation Bible School. The youth minister should seek out tables where only adults are sitting at church events, or sit in worship with his or her family instead of the youth pew. There is a whole congregation that can (and should) be encouraged to sit with youth during church functions.

116

# CHAPTER 7
# WAYS TO ADD INTEGRATION INTO YOUR CHURCH'S MINISTRIES

*I look upon all the world as my parish; thus far I
mean, than in whatever part of it I am, I judge it
meet, right, and my bounden duty to declare, unto all
that are willing to hear, the glad tidings of salvation.
This is the work which I know God has called me
to. And sure I am that His blessing attends it.*
— John Wesley

Many may wish to jump straight to this chapter and start
implementing these strategies and ideas for integration without
reading the rest of the book. How do I know that? Because
I do the same thing with lots of books that include a more
pragmatic section. I often skip the "why" and jump to the
"how." After all, I must already be on board with the "why"
because I bought the book in the first place, right? The problem
with this approach is that it takes more than one person starting
new programs to integrate a church. You must be able to fully
explain the "why" in order to get staff and leadership on board
with the new focus, and it's important to recognize pitfalls and
barriers that may hinder the process of integrating your youth
with the whole congregation.

If you must, start by taking a look at the ideas in this chapter.
Let them move you and inspire ideas and dreams of your

own. Then go back and read the other chapters. Hand the book to some of your church leaders and the heads of various ministries. Let others recognize the benefits and sustainability of bringing youth into the life of your whole congregation. Help others share the vision of a church family that supports and seeks out the growth and strength of the community as a whole.

The main reason for this chapter isn't just to list ideas of new ministries where you can involve youth. Remember, what we're talking about isn't something a program or curriculum can fix. I list ideas in this chapter mainly to get you thinking about ministries in your church that are outside of your youth programming, and to help you come up with ways for the youth to collaborate with the adults who already do those ministries. As you read through these suggestions and ideas, let them spark in you a new way of looking at your youth in the church. Think about how you'd go about intentionally involving teenagers in your church ministries for the sake of strengthening the body of Christ that is your congregation.

I've divided these various strategies into four areas of ministry that exist (or should exist) in every church—worship, hospitality/fellowship, service/outreach, and discipleship. Most areas of ministry will fall under at least one of these headings. Administration might be separate, but I've placed those ideas into service as well. After all, we're called to serve not only those outside the community, but also each other. By focusing on these areas, a church can be involved in youth ministry even if there are no teenagers in the congregation.[33]

## WORSHIP

Corporate worship is perhaps the easiest and quickest way to bring integration into the faith community. A worship service should be where people of all ages congregate and join together in song and story, lifting prayers and praises to God. Doing this together as one body helps to strengthen ties, form relationships, build memories, and foster awareness of each other. Granted, worship that is dry and uninteresting could alienate more than just the youth of the church, but when the congregation participates together in the life of worship, the service becomes alive and exciting. It becomes the words and actions of a people of faith. When youth are brought into the mix—leading, singing, serving—the experience enriches adults, children, and youth alike.

## All Together Now!
Although worship with the entire congregation works best for integration, there are some churches where this isn't possible in the near future. That's no reason to skip over this section of ideas. If your youth worship separately from the rest of the congregation, you'll have to work three times harder to get them connected with people outside the youth ministry silo. You can look for ways to bring a few of your youth into the main worship setting and also bring adults into the youth worship space and time. Work hard to make the worship planning and leadership a two-way street—where youth will cross over and help lead the adult worship and where adults (who aren't already youth workers) will mentor the youth worship team and contribute at times to the youth worship.

## Yes, Every Week
Providing a Sunday morning once or twice a year for the youth to shine in worship might be a great way to remind the rest of the congregation that the youth are a part of the church, but it doesn't get the youth involved with other leaders and volunteers. In fact, in many ways, it only strengthens the silo. Rather than simply planning a Youth Sunday every now and then, regularly include youth to serve alongside the adults in the rotation of those who help in worship. Recruit a few youth who will serve each month on the usher crew; allow some

capable youth to read or recite Scripture from memory; invite youth with musical interests to offer special music or to play with the regular musicians. If there is a worship committee in your church, invite teenagers to sit in on the planning meetings for an upcoming preaching series or season. Each of these worship collaborations will engage youth with church adults who can either coach them or serve alongside. When this is done regularly, relationships will develop and grow.

## Visual Arts

We are all artisans, according to Erwin McManus. He believes "we all need to create, to be a part of a process that brings to the world something beautiful, good, and true, in order to allow our souls to come to life."[34] Human beings are created in the image of God, and an essential part of that image is creating beauty.

Help your congregation recognize the beauty of creativity by encouraging your youth to offer artistic visual expressions in the worship space. Even traditional sanctuaries can bring in creative themes on the altar, banners, bulletin covers, posters, or displays that will help the congregation focus on the theme for the worship service. Worship slide backgrounds, architectural models, sculptures, video, and typography might also be useful in illuminating some part of the Scripture or message.

Wanda, an adult member of First UMC in Lancaster, Ohio, enjoyed liturgical dance. One year Wanda met with the new confirmation class and helped the students create a liturgical expression of a song for the main worship service. But what was unique about this situation was that Wanda was in her 80s. I was skeptical at first, certain that the boys in the class wouldn't go for any kind of physical expression of worship in public—especially if it had any similarity to dance.

As they worked on it over the weeks, though, the students got to know Wanda. She not only showed them how to create and remember the liturgical dance, but she shared much of her story and her passion for God. By the end of their time together, the youth (including the boys) had created something beautiful to share in worship and had built a relationship with an older church leader. Wanda also enjoyed experiencing the youthful joy of creativity in worship. The following year she invited her friend Chuck to join her as a small group leader with the next confirmation class.

Create a visual worship collaboration between youth and adults to express upcoming worship themes or a particular season such as Advent or Lent. Who in your church enjoys making beautiful things? Do you know some quilters? Let them show some teens how to make a quilt that tells a story pertaining to the Scripture used in a sermon. Those who sew can help youth create banners; a woodworker or carpenter can show youth how to make a manger, a cross, a table, or another object that helps illustrate the worship story. When you start this kind of hands-on worship connection, your youth and adults will begin dreaming of more ways they can create visuals for worship.

## Drama
Why limit drama and skits to youth gatherings and talent shows? Many youth love to perform on the stage; allow them to use their gifts to glorify God and direct people to the gospel. You will need to work far in advance of a Sunday message so you can find (or create) the proper script and have the time to cast and practice it. But as one skit is completed, youth can start focusing on the next one a month or so ahead. Again, use your congregation to help direct the youth in this. If you have adults who enjoy directing or writing, use them in the production and scriptwriting. If you want props, use some builders and artists for scene work (adults as well as youth). If you need costumes, connect a few youth with seamstresses

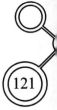

or people who like to frequent used clothing stores. The benefit here is twofold: linking youth with creative adults and introducing youth creativity in the congregational worship space.

A drama ministry like this can quickly take up too much time for the youth minister. Find a few adults in your community who enjoy drama—some who are creative with props and scenery and others who like to direct or produce. Before you know it, you will have a drama team that mixes ages and works collaboratively with your worship planners in bringing the gospel to the entire congregation.

## Tech
Dramas and skits can also be presented in video form for worship. Using video allows for soundtrack and scene changes as well as editing and other production elements that aren't usually involved in short stage or live presentations. Often it's the youth who are on the cutting edge of video and presentation technologies. Invite them to help design the media arts for a single upcoming service (background screen images, music, short video clips) or bring them in as weekly volunteers on the video/tech team.

However, it's important to ask youth to do this in ways beyond simply pushing a button or bringing up the sound or the lights in the service. Students interested in video or tech are capable of doing more than pushing buttons. Give them permission to be creative. When youth are allowed to create content for worship—when they are a part of the creative focus of bringing praise to God—they will connect more with the message and with the congregation. When youth are paired with adults in the creation of such visuals, they will connect worship and the faith story with members of the congregation. Stories and worship become reliant on one another. Community is nurtured. Faith is grounded on an experience with the body of Christ.

## Music

Some of your church's best musicians might be youth, and they can be a substantial blessing to your music ministry. Those who sing in school choirs or play in the school band rehearse their skills daily. While many churches use music-minded youth in worship, not as many incorporate youth into the regular church praise band or chancel choir. Usually you will see a youth praise band or a youth choir offering up the musical leadership on an occasional Sunday more often than you'll find one or two youth regularly joining in with the band or choir each week. What would happen if your choir or praise band were to intentionally include teens in their ranks? Imagine the relationships built between the generations when youth are brought into the regular practice—the prayers, the laughter and jokes, the planning and successes.

The church choir is often a very supportive group of Christians in a congregation—praying for each other, discussing the worship services, and offering help and care in times of need. Including teens in such a community will bring new levels of mentorship and discipleship to the adults and youth involved. Those youth who are invited into this kind of worship leadership would be much more likely to continue to support the band or choir into adulthood.

Justin was a shy eighth grade boy who didn't connect all that well to the youth in the church. He attended a different school than everyone else and was busy most weekends. The thing he was busy with, though, was his violin. He loved to play and was very good at it. When the youth minister discovered the praise band was seeking someone to play fiddle for a song they planned to play in a few weeks, he arranged for Justin to join in the rehearsals. It went so well that Justin started playing each Sunday during the main worship time. He gained enough confidence to attend a youth ministry breakfast each week (partly because he got to know and trust the youth minister), but his main love and focus became worship because he was offering a part of himself—something he was passionate about—to God in worship. The relationships Justin built with the band members through practice and leading worship also helped him to experience the whole congregation and not just the youth ministry.

## Up Close and Personal
Try talking your youth into sitting together in the front row during worship for a season. Their presence may change the whole dynamic of worship and the congregation.

When the youth at Hickory Flat UMC moved to the front row, it had that effect. The congregation paid attention to the youth and the ways they worshipped, the youth were more attentive to what happened in worship, the worship team thought more about ways they could lead the youth in worship, and even the pastor started organizing his messages with the youth in mind. This didn't happen intentionally, though. Like many who prepare messages, the pastor would imagine the faces in the congregation that he usually saw from the pulpit. As the youth were now sitting in his field of vision (instead of in the back row or out in the youth room), he began imagining their response each time he prepared a sermon—each time he prayed for his congregation. The youth were even seen dancing to certain songs because the front row has more room than any other seat in the sanctuary.

# HOSPITALITY/FELLOWSHIP
"Hospitality has been interpreted in many ways, but…true hospitality comes from the heart without expectation of anything in return…it is not genuine if done only with the goal of gaining profit."[35]

Involving youth in the hospitality ministry of your church places them with other church members who have a heart of servanthood. Teenagers will quickly discover how effective hospitality is in bringing happiness and comfort to others. Some opportunities for hospitality involve interaction with people, while others are more behind the scenes. And yet both offer a message that is primary to the body of Christ: "You are welcome here."

## Meet & Greet

The people who volunteer to be greeters at your church must have a deep love for the community. They ought to know where things are, understand how things run, and know many of the people who attend. These are great people for your youth to know (and great for them to know the youth). How cool would it be if you had five or six youth who rotated through the greeter team, working with adults and participating fully in the ministry of welcome? Those youth would experience faith from the perspective of volunteers who make a point to tell others about their church.

If your church doesn't have a greeter ministry, it's not difficult to start one. It does involve a team of people who are willing to hold doors, smile a lot, and quickly find answers to questions. A greeter must tend to the little details that help people feel welcome. But help the team understand that the purpose of a greeter isn't to bring more people into the church. As all of us are called to do, a greeter is simply showing the love of Christ to everyone he or she meets.

A greeter is often the first person a visitor meets, so it's a good idea to find friendly, informed church members. Once you have your team, add a few youth to the mix. Include them in planning and training meetings, helping them get to know the other greeters through a mixer that invites people to tell a bit about their story. The sooner your youth volunteers get to know these people, the sooner they, too, will feel more welcomed into their church family.

## Tour Guides

What if your church were to offer a tour of its campus on Sunday mornings after the morning worship services? Whether the church is a big campus or a tiny building, all churches have a history, and there are always stories to tell about the building, the congregation, and the church's presence in the community. Whatever there may be to show people, the tour is made more remarkable by the guides who help the visitors feel welcome and comfortable. Adults and youth should plan and carry out these tours together. As the tour partners plan and discuss the way they will guide, they get to know one another in new ways. As they talk more about the ministries they are involved in, each gains a deeper love and appreciation for his or her congregation.

## Comfort Food

A funeral is a time when families and compassion connect. The community of faith joins together to offer care for the bereaved and help in times of mourning. What a wonderful way to experience and witness the love and compassion of the body of Christ. Such love and outreach will make an impact on youth if they can find some way to be involved.

If your church doesn't already have a ministry of providing meals for funerals, consider starting one. This is a great ministry for a congregation that tends to be older, as more funerals will take place in this community and youth will gain an understanding and appreciation for helping in this time of loss. A funeral meal ministry is the preparation and serving of a meal for the family and guests of the departed following the funeral. It's an opportunity for friends and relatives to gather and support each other, sharing memories and catching up with one another. The church offers the place and the food for such a gathering, serving as a quiet host for the family and friends. To help keep the cost low, congregation members donate homemade dishes and serve behind the scenes, setting out the food, pouring drinks, and cleaning up afterward. A donation is generally expected from the family of the departed to help defer the costs of the ministry.

This ministry should be open to church members of all ages. Youth and children can help in the kitchen alongside adults, but even the planning and pre-meal duties can be carried out by the youth. The more a teenager experiences the compassion and presence of Christ in action, the more he or she will express compassion to others in adulthood.

## Video Story

A valuable project for your youth would be to create a video highlighting your church—its ministries and people. Imagine a few of your teenagers interviewing some of your long-time church members, talking about their memories and stories, hearing about the ministries they've enjoyed and why they like being active in the church. Youth can plan, edit, and produce this video, using pictures, interviews, and historical accounts telling the story of the church's past and present involvement in your community. Your youth will learn more about their congregation, build relationships with those they interview, and understand what makes their church the right fit for them. The resulting video can be placed in the church archives or shown to visitors and new members, but the greater end result will be a fostered care and appreciation for the congregation and its presence in the community.

## Website

Go to your church website. What do you see? What do you not see that should be there? Can someone who has never been to your church find important information—street address, a phone number, the name of the pastor, a picture of the building,

and the times of some of the main events like worship, Sunday school, and youth group?

Your church's presence on the web is one way to communicate to visitors that they are welcome here! If your church doesn't have a website (or one that's up to date), how about creating a web team that's in charge of planning the site and keeping it updated? Some churches hire a professional web design company, but most use volunteers in the church (or just one lonely volunteer at a desktop) to make their presence known on the web. And some simply put up a site when the church first got Internet service and haven't touched it since, expecting the Holy Spirit to make any necessary changes.

Involve your youth in the web ministry of your church. Put some youth to work on some of the ministry pages. Their task should involve talking with those in charge of the ministries, posting general information, announcing special upcoming events, and keeping the pages up to date. They should keep the look of the pages consistent throughout the site, maintaining a cohesive look and message that represents your church.

Remember that the point of this ministry is twofold: first, it gets the word out on the Internet so anyone can find out about your church and its ministries; and second, it creates opportunities for youth interaction with other ministries in your church.

## Childcare

Parents love to talk about their kids. Volunteers who take care of children will naturally develop relationships with families in the church. Bring some of your older teenagers into volunteer status with the church nursery, but be sure they're not allowed to work alone. Adults should be in charge—for safety and legal reasons, as well as for opportunities of integration. Here is a perfect setting for intergenerational relationships between children and the youth and adults who watch over them.

Choose teenagers who relate well with children. In my years of doing youth ministry in local churches, there were always a few youth who gravitated toward helping in the nursery. Sometimes they were active in our youth ministry programs, but often they worked in the nursery because they didn't want to go to worship or Sunday school. The amazing thing is, once those youth became young adults, they almost always continued to be involved in the church (or joined a church elsewhere once they moved away). Youth who helped in the nursery found a sense of belonging in community with the whole church in ways that other youth hadn't found by simply being involved in the youth programming.

Helping in the nursery also gave youth a certain confidence and comfort level around young children. Years later, I've found that nursery work turned out to be good, basic parent training for youth who are now adults raising their own kids.

## SERVICE/OUTREACH

Jesus was very clear in calling his followers to serve one another. In John 13, Jesus washes his disciples' feet and tells them that since he has served them, they are to serve one another. He also tells his disciples that the first must be last—must become the least among them. When you guide your youth into areas of service in your church community, you will help them not only get to know their fellow congregants, but also be the very presence of Christ to those they serve.

### Committees

Who would have thought a book about youth ministry would encourage you to get your youth involved in church committees? I've heard some church members compare committee meetings to torture. While youth ministry looks for

creative ways to teach and experience the gospel, a committee meeting is mostly just...a meeting.

Recall Jesus' words—in order to experience the kingdom of God, we must become like children. Youth are generally thought of as older than children, but they still have some of the childlike qualities that can help your committee members and church leadership experience the kingdom. Why would we want to keep their insights and ideas away from our planning and decision making? Your leadership can learn much about the kingdom by incorporating youth into some church meetings.

I'm not recommending that you simply nominate a teenager to serve on a committee and then throw him or her in for a quadrennium of service. Take care to find a mentor on the council or committee who can take an interest in the teenager— someone who can help recognize the gifts and graces that youth have for such service. Set up an intentional leadership learning experience for youth who serve on committees, pairing them with key adults and helping them focus on the church's calling in the community. Youth in leadership positions can be paired with adults who will "shadow" the youth, helping them fit into the leadership to which they are called and gifted. It is only in the proper training of younger church leaders and passing on the leadership torch that a church and its ministries can continue to thrive.

## Mission Trips

Perhaps the best single experience your youth can have for faith development is one of service—especially a short-term mission trip where they leave the comforts and expectations of normal life and step into something and someplace uncomfortable. Serving outside our comfort zone pushes us to rely on something that is more reliable than familiar surroundings—it encourages us to rely on God. A mission field can be far away, leaving any semblance of familiarity. Or it can be just around the corner, viewing a familiar neighborhood through the lens of service.

Jesus said of serving others in their needs, "Whatever you did for one of the least of these brothers and sisters of mine, you did for me" (Matthew 25:40). A mission or service experience allows us to come face-to-face with the Christ. Sometimes we might not recognize him in the homeless person we feed or the prisoner we visit, but any encounter with the Christ is bound to change us. In serving, we also become the embodiment—the very presence—of the Christ to others. Being a vessel through whom Jesus reaches out is transformational for the one serving.

Youth groups often plan and participate in mission trips, but what would happen if your church invited people of all ages to take the opportunity to encounter and embody the Christ together? Imagine the bonding and growth that could occur between adults and youth and even children as they serve Christ by serving strangers.

Even more important than integration during the mission trip is the way you involve youth in the pre-trip planning. Do you want music on your mission trip? Invite a youth who plays guitar. Let him or her plan the songs and the worship times with a few adults and the pastor. If you don't have many musicians, bring in a few recorded playlists of approved songs for the trip, but make sure a youth and adult work together on forming these song mixes. The music played on the trip will represent the mix of generations involved in service.

Do you know what kind of work you'll be doing as you serve? Ask youth to come up with the supplies needed or take them on a scouting trip to view the site ahead of time (if practical). Use youth to plan meals, tend to the details of worship plans, work on communication with the church while away through blogs or social media, organize the work day, and plan activities or morale-boosting surprises along the route to and from the location. The more involved the youth are in the planning of a ministry, the more ownership is built and relationships are developed for years of sustainable ministry.

## Kitchen

Daryl was a teenager who joined a local church after his parents divorced. He participated in the youth ministries right away, but he wouldn't have known many other church members if he'd stayed involved with just the youth. One night Daryl's mom asked him to step into the kitchen and help wash dishes during a church dinner. It was a last-minute substitution, but he was willing to do it. In the kitchen he discovered a team of fun, service-loving people (children and adults alike) who were pretty easy to get to know. He also found that he enjoyed greeting people at the window as they handed him their dirty dishes. Soon many people knew Daryl, and he gained an appreciation for his church as more than just a place to meet for youth group. Church became a diverse group of people who loved Daryl as a part of their faith family.

## Congregational Care

So many church ministries fall under the umbrella of congregational care that it possibly should be its own heading separate from service. Congregational care will help your youth recognize their value to the entire church because it connects them with people in need whom they will rub elbows with even after that need is met. It is important that such ministries be done in partnership with other adult members in the church. Here are some suggestions that may even spark other new ideas in including your youth in congregational care:

- Visiting the homebound or sick

- Making care packages for church missionaries or

students away at college

- Delivering meals to new parents

- Praying for leaders in the church

- Praying for church members with urgent needs

- Making prayer blankets

- Serving coffee on Sunday mornings

# DISCIPLESHIP

I've heard it stated time and again that the youth are not the church of tomorrow, but they are the church of today. If that is true, then they should be involved in the mission of the church—to make disciples. If we wait until tomorrow to involve youth in the task of the church, then it might never happen.

This command of Christ to make disciples can be carried out in many ways, and the way the youth make disciples might look very different from the way adults do it. Making disciples together and sharing in that vision will be effective in bringing the youth out of a silo mentality and into the mission of the whole church.

Most of the suggestions that fit under discipleship are appropriate and perfect for churches who claim they don't have any youth (and, therefore, think they have no reason to have a youth ministry). All of us are called to be in ministry with youth in some way or another. If your church (or a church down the road from you) has no youth in attendance, use these ideas and some of your own as ways to reach out and disciple youth in your community. Remember that the purpose should not be to get them into your church but to be the presence of the Christ and communicate the gospel. Such a presence in discipleship will certainly bring transformation—possibly for the youth, but always for the one who is being the presence of Jesus.

## Finding Mentors

John Sowers, president of The Mentoring Project, often says, "This generation has been wounded the most in relationships—it is in relationships where the healing must begin."[36]

Building sustainable relationships is what mentoring is all about. When you bring mentoring into your church community, you help adults intentionally focus on the social, moral, and faith development of young people.

True mentors are chosen by the mentees. A young person recognizes something in an older, more experienced individual that will help that young person grow or learn, and then he or she chooses or names the person who will serve as a mentor. In the church, however, it's often done the other way around. A mentor is often pointed in the direction of a teenager through a program or ministry. Sometimes the youth doesn't even know the adult mentor. Once the relationship is started, it will succeed if the youth allows the interaction to bring change.

There are a number of ways to help adults in the church begin a mentoring attitude. I've listed a few ideas for you below.

Help an adult Sunday school class, men's or women's group, or Bible study "adopt" a few youth from your congregation. Be specific about who you connect them to, giving pertinent contact information that the parents of the teenager provides. (Name, age, birthdate, address, school, grade—but make sure you have parent permission before giving this information out to anyone.) Ask the class members to commit to praying for this student by name daily and to making sure that someone in the class is in touch with the student at least once a week. When the youth is seen at church by anyone in the class, they must make a point to approach and engage him or her in conversation (not everyone at once, of course!). You may wish to do this for a limited time at first, like during Lent or throughout the summer months. People are more willing to take on a new practice if it has a clear beginning and ending. Then, if it goes well, do it again or ask participants to carry it on longer.

Connect individual mentors when young people enter into the youth ministry program. Many churches do this as a part of the confirmation process, but it can be incorporated in the first year of being involved in the youth ministry department. Ask the youth if there are any adults in the church whom they would like to invite to be a mentor. Explain that a mentor agrees to pray for the student daily, connect with the student at least once a week (through e-mail, texting, phone, or face-to-face contact), read a gospel together, worship a few times during the year together, and get together over a meal or snack at least once a month. If the youth can think of no one to recommend, then find the adult yourself.

The church should screen any of these mentor connections, making sure to connect youth only with adults who know how to have appropriate relationships with teenagers. Explain to the adult what is expected of him or her as a mentor (sometimes called Friend in Faith), and plant the possibility of this relationship continuing until the youth goes away to college or moves away (with fewer responsibilities after the first year). In my experience, some of these connections have continued on for years, including mentors being invited to weddings or becoming sponsors at a baby's baptism.

Interest-based mentoring can also foster strong relationships between adults and youth. While growing up in our church in Ohio, my son Jesse was involved in a black-light theater ministry. As a young teenager, he was doing ministry with a mixture of children, older youth, young adults, and older adults. The connections through this ministry fostered care and oversight for the children and youth involved. Later, Jesse started taking private trombone lessons from a church member. He thrived from the encouragement and tutoring of this older adult who would talk with him and acknowledge him on Sunday mornings at worship. Years later, Jesse built a relationship with an engineer at church when he started needing help with his senior project that focused on architecture. All of these connections helped Jesse view his church as a support and guide for his growth and development. In the process of talking about those shared interests, he heard faith stories and witnessed worship from those he admired along the way.

Adult volunteers can make a difference simply by showing up for youth events outside the church, offering support and encouragement to the youth and families involved. This kind of ministry should include adults who might not usually work with the youth. In fact, if a church were to do this well, there might be no need for planning regular youth ministry programs. Your church members who connect with the youth will discover and design ways to get together. There are many adults in a congregation who love the theater or enjoy helping at sports meets or cheering at football games. Let these adults know the youth who are performing in the next play, who runs on the track team, who plays in the band at halftime at the game, or who is on the local school's football or basketball team. Encourage those adults to step out and make their presence known at these events, sitting with parents at games, volunteering at practices, or simply saying "hi" and "good job" at the events. Then, on Sunday morning, bring up the play or the game or the event again, showing support and encouragement.

Canton First UMC has set up a ministry that helps connect youth with older church members through home visits. These aren't necessarily shut-ins, but adults in the church who have very little connection to the youth ministry. There is no agenda for these visits except to build connections between people who might not get to know each other. Suggest that the youth make conversation about collections or displays in the home, pictures of family, the youth's school activities, ministries each person enjoys, trips each have taken, and even the fun topic of what things have changed or stayed the same since the adult was a teenager. Youth generally come away from the experience with greater confidence in their ability to converse with people they may not know well, and adults realize they may have more in common with teenagers than they originally thought.

## College Connections

What happens to a student in your church after they've come through the children's and youth ministries? Does the youth who is now a young adult stay involved in your church? If students move away to college, do they join a church or campus ministry while away at school?

Some of you who work with youth might be saying ever so quietly in the back of your mind, "I'm just thankful someone else has the responsibility for them once they head to college."

Even if your church has a staff person working in college-age ministries, the congregation has a responsibility to find ways to support and connect with these young adults. Ministry, service, and discipleship can and should continue after high school, and making it happen will be a wonderful discipleship experience for your congregation.

Try setting up a mentor-like relationship with each student as he or she goes to college—either through a Sunday school class, men's or women's group, a Bible study, or individual

adults. Ask these people to write regularly to students (especially through snail mail). You might even hint that college students love homemade cookies. Wouldn't it be powerful if these mentor relationships were a continuation of the ones that began when the youth first entered middle school? If your church is located near a college or university, look for ways to become an affiliate congregation—someplace that students can feel at home while they're away from their true home church. You can give students encouragement and confidence in their young adulthood by giving them a place to continue to grow in faith. Be in communication with the home churches and intentionally pursue the college students, helping them connect with your congregation. Statistics show that if a student doesn't connect with a congregation or a college ministry within the first two weeks of college, chances are he or she never will.

Ask your congregation to pray regularly for each college student. List them by name in the bulletin, newsletter, or on the video screen during worship. Praying for individuals by name brings the body of Christ closer together. Be certain to let the student know that he or she is being prayed for. Care like this should never be a secret.

Visit colleges with your youth in their senior year of high school. You could plan a short road trip where you and a vanload of college-bound students visit five or six schools. Introduce these youth to some local church pastors, to the campus chaplains, and to some of the campus ministries. Take pictures and bring them back to share with the parents and your congregation. While it's likely that many students will select colleges farther away and may not attend any of these colleges you visit as a group, visiting a college as a youth group activity will help youth in this transition feel more comfortable seeking out and attending a campus ministry or church once they arrive at the college of choice.

Start a class for high school seniors as they prepare for new responsibilities in young adulthood. Schedule guest speakers from your church membership who can teach the class responsible Christian practices like working with a budget, determining your vocation, leadership and servanthood, social settings at college, and finding a church or faith connection. You could even bring in church members to teach practical skills like cooking, car care, and home repair.

## Prayer Partners

Incredible things happen in a community of people who pray for one another. After a sermon or message about prayer or caring for the young, announce an opportunity for church members to sign up to be a prayer partner with a teenager. Those youth who agree to participate (through registration forms with signed parental consent) are given 3x5 cards to fill out with their names, a picture, and helpful information— birthdate, age, grade, school, and hobbies they may enjoy. The adults are encouraged to pick up a card and commit to pray for the youth daily for a certain season. (I've seen this done during Lent, Advent, the summer, or in the fall as kids head back to school.) It's important keep a list of the partnerships, as you can contact the prayer partners to notify them of special prayer requests or major events in each other's lives.

For extra impact, the youth could also pray for the adult so the prayers go both ways between the generations. God does amazing things in relationships when we pray for someone daily for a number of weeks.

## Pen Pals

On a recent mission trip to the Bahamas, I was with a group of high school youth who received letters each day from church members. There were hundreds of letters. Each of the 25 people on the trip received at least one letter a day (sometimes more). Letters came from parents and family, from friends, or

from church members who knew them well, but some letters came from someone the recipients didn't even know. Adults and children in the church wrote letters to individual youth to assure them of their prayers, to express their thankfulness for the way God was using them, and to share their hopes for the deepening faith experiences of these short-term missionaries.

Retreats and camp experiences are often the most powerful faith experiences in a young person's life. Church members can share in that experience and be a part of the memory even if they aren't physically there. A month or two before a youth retreat or summer camp, start getting in touch with some significant adults in the church (or some children) whose "presence through the pen" would communicate a caring and thoughtful witness to the students on the trip.

A connection like this is especially valuable for children and youth who go away to a summer camp, as a church camping experience focuses on helping participants recognize God's love in their lives and in their communities. Camp staff spend their energy and resources all week to help campers know and experience God, and connecting this new awareness with the church family back home would affirm their belonging in the body of Christ in both settings.

Look for other ways your church can be a presence at camps and retreats. Adopt a camp staff person for the summer and send him or her weekly gifts (mmm, cookies!) and notes of support; write a letter to a cabin group, telling them that your class is praying for them by name; send gifts that will be handed out to the cabin group or to the entire camp— something that will connect the theme of the week with the gospel.

These camp connections don't necessarily have to be for youth from your own church, as any connections made in this way help to broaden the scope of the local church, strengthening the understanding of what it means to be the church in the world.

# CHAPTER 8
# A CHRONICLER OF GRACE: THE YOUTH MINISTER AS AN AGENT OF INTEGRATION

*"When you teach," she said, instructing me, "I learn something for the day.... But when you preach—" she lowered her voice and probed me the deeper with her eyes—"God is here. And sometimes he's smiling," she said, "and sometimes he is frowning surely."*
— Walter Wangerin,
*Miz Lil and the Chronicles of Grace*

All of this focus on integration and collaboration between church ministries doesn't mean we have to reinvent the ministries within our churches. It does mean, though, that someone should help the congregation and the staff focus on ways God can use each of us to connect with each other as the body of Christ. The youth minister is one of the best-prepared persons for this task.

If you read *Redefining the Role of the Youth Worker: A Manifesto of Integration* by April Diaz, you'll find a description of how Newsong Church in Irvine, California, created a job description for a student integration pastor, rather than hire another youth minister. Mike Park was hired to fill the position, and I met him at The Summit 2012, a youth ministry conference of The Youth Cartel. Mike talked about his job at Newsong and how it differs from that of a traditional youth minister. He spends a lot of time shining a spotlight on what God is doing with teenagers in the various ministries at the church, as well as within families, in the schools, and beyond. He helps youth and adults collaborate in finding "the best ways to connect, engage, and champion the movement of God together."[37]

I like what Mike says about what happened when he first started his job and how he thought he had to reinvent the church's youth ministry. "That line of thinking falls into the same trap of trying to build a better youth ministry, rather than seeing the whole church as a place for meaningful relationships and spiritual formation for teenagers and families. Instead of innovative programming that specifically targets student integration, we work on making everything we do part of our student integration vision."[38] When a congregation sees that it's better together than apart, then integration can become a clearer and easier priority.

It's easy to fall back into what Mark Oestreicher describes as Youth Ministry 2.0, a program-driven model of youth ministry.[39] But we youth ministers must stop continually trying to become "better" with new programming and instead enable our congregations to safely navigate the "turn in the track." Help members see opportunities that already exist for integration, become familiar with the many ministries within the church, and connect people through stories of God's work in the community.

## HELP OTHERS SEE OPPORTUNITIES

Being an agent of integration in your church means recognizing opportunities for connection and helping the community adapt to the change in direction. Sometimes that change is severe and involves loss; sometimes change is smooth and celebratory and we wonder why we've never done it before. Always change is going to take some getting used to, as it moves away from the way you've always done things and finds God at work in some new and remarkable ways.

The youth minister is often the right person to point out those remarkable ways that God is involved in the change. While the church may not need to change the job description of the youth minister so it describes a youth integration pastor, I encourage all involved in youth ministry to work feverishly at changing the mind-set of the congregation, moving parents, church leaders, and even youth away from the notion that the youth ministry leaders (professional as well as volunteer) are the only ones responsible to journey with teenagers on their faith walk. Become a signpost for opportunities in your community; promote activities and events where adults can connect with youth; direct church members to greet youth each time they see them (especially when they see them in the community); and encourage suggestions of other ways to be the presence of Christ to teenagers in your church.

## GET TO KNOW THE MINISTRIES—ALL OF THEM

In order to make good connections, a youth minister should become familiar with the ministries in the church and see them with new eyes. I used to sit in church staff meetings and listen to the plans for different ministries, grateful they existed but also thankful that some of those programs or activities weren't my responsibility. Unless I considered them relevant to youth ministry, I would sort of check out of the meeting until it was my turn to share about my upcoming youth events. Not only was that unhelpful as a team member, but it totally fed into the silo that I'd helped create at my church. Why would a teenager look toward the whole church for opportunities of growth in faith if the youth minister and the rest of the church staff weren't even going there?

Each area of ministry should be able to name a way it can collaborate with youth—not because your youth need to experience quilting or running a church barbecue, but any activity outside of their youth silo will get them involved with others in the body of Christ. It gets the "eye" to appreciate the "belly." (I'll let you figure out which one is which.)

Chuck Foster reminds us that the places and times for the nurturing of relationships exist in many of the events on your church calendar. He says when we purposefully turn to our church-wide events as opportunities for education and faith growth, the events "become catalysts to the informal and formal conversations that bind, in turn, the diversity of a congregation's children, youth, and adults into a community of faith."[40] The congregation moves from divided generations to an interdependence that nurtures their faith through the years.

The interdependence I'm referring to shouldn't translate to extra tasks for the youth minister. Quite the opposite. Once youth connect with other church members and find their place in other ministries, the youth minister becomes less of an event planner and more of a connector between ministries and people. Imagine your youth coming home from a mission trip all fired up for service and joining the church's mission committee to help plan a church-wide, intergenerational mission trip for the next year. Imagine youth who lead music in worship asking to partner with the VBS team. The next time you're sitting in a staff meeting and you hear about an upcoming painting project or the Sunday morning parking team, suggest a few youth who can work together with those in charge.

And I'm not talking about the common mind-set at some staff and committee meetings of "Get some of the youth to do it." What we're talking about here is a collaboration between youth and adults and, in some cases, children.

# DISCOVER AND CONNECT THE STORIES

As you focus more attention on ministries in your church—the ones outside the youth department—you will hopefully meet individuals who support those ministries and get to know how God can use them. The talents of the lady who is leading music at VBS would be great to share with some of the youth who also love music or teach sign language. But it would also be impressive if you could share the story of her involvement in campus ministry when she was in college. She would be a great resource for your small group of senior girls. The story of the head usher's struggle with the loss of his son to cancer would really connect with Kyle and Travis who are dealing with some loss of their own. Jessica would be motivated to act boldly when she hears about how Mr. Jackson found an eye doctor willing to donate his or her services for a partially blind girl he met on a recent trip overseas. Rachel would be empowered to keep her baby when she realizes a group of parents are ready to step up and support her because that's what others did for them when they needed it. Connections like these will require you to get to know people outside the youth ministry so you can be an effective agent of integration.

Walter Wangerin Jr. is a gifted storyteller. In his book *Miz Lil and the Chronicles of Grace*, he shows us the importance of being chroniclers of God's grace in and around our own communities.[41] At a conference in Chicago, I heard him tell youth ministers to be in tune with where God is breaking in and with how God offers grace in our communities. He called us to point others to those times and instances, connecting the grace of the God of Scripture with the grace of the God of your people. A chronicler of grace retells the stories from the community so everyone can experience God's connection with one another.

The best ways you can connect your community stories with

your church members is by learning them, and the best way to learn them is by listening and paying attention to each individual—recognizing that *everyone* has a story. God is pursuing all of us, and each person (though he or she may not know it) plays a part in the story of God's grace.

People of all ages love story time! What if you were to start telling some stories of God's grace in your community as a closing devotion or during worship time with your youth? As the chronicler of God's grace, you could tell stories you've heard (with permission from the story subject) during a youth function or at a particular gathering each month (like the first youth meeting of each month). After a while, youth and leaders will understand what you're doing and will begin opening their own ears for these stories. Soon they may also open their mouths to speak these stories aloud in similar settings.

A great resource for learning stories is by talking to the parents of your youth. A parent loves to talk about a son or daughter. Sitting with parents during a football game or track meet gives you plenty of time to listen, and it also shows parents you're interested in connecting during these teenage years. Communicate to those parents that you and the other youth leaders are committed to supporting them in the faith development of their children.

# CHAPTER 9
# ALL CHURCHES SHOULD BE DOING YOUTH MINISTRY

*May the adoption of this beloved child be blessed.*
*Almighty God, you adopted your people in*
*Egypt, and they came out into the wilderness to*
*pitch a tent. May we the family of this beloved*
*child enjoy the presence of God in the tent of life*
*together as we look toward the pillar of fire by*
*day—a sign of your coming glorious redemption.*
*And the pillar of cloud by night—a sign of your*
*presence amid our trials and darkness.*
— A Prayer for Adoption,
*Common Prayer: A Liturgy for Ordinary Radicals*

I serve as a youth and young adult resource person to the
United Methodist Churches in North Georgia. I love meeting
with pastors, parent groups, youth ministry leadership teams,
and search committees to talk about ways we can help each
other.

Every now and then I hear a pastor say, "We don't have any
youth in our church, so we don't really need to talk about how
to do youth ministry."

Really?

Is that how you interpret the commission Christ gave us?

What if the first disciples were to say, "We don't have any Gentiles, so we don't really need to reach out to them"? What if Abraham and Sarah had said, "We don't have any children, so we don't need so much land"?

A statement like this is just as siloed as a huge church whose youth have nothing to do with the rest of the church. If we think the only way to do youth ministry is with the youth who come through our church doors, then we are grossly misunderstanding our calling as a Christian community. We renew our faith and reclaim our identity by passing it on to the young—in our church, in our community, and in the world. In that way, children and youth help us experience the kingdom here on earth. "Forming faith in congregations can only be renewed, consequently, as it is also transformed."[42]

In a way, having no youth in your church frees you up even more to experience this kind of relational, incarnational youth ministry. There is no youth ministry silo in the church if there is no activity planned for youth. The youth ministry in a church where there are no youth is all about relationships. It reaches out and sits with youth where they are, simply for the purpose of spending time with them (and not to bring them to church or create a youth ministry). Teenagers can spot a hidden agenda from miles away. So when they know they aren't being recruited for your youth program, a conversation with an adult church member will have more impact.

We are heirs with Christ through adoption as children of God. Likewise, people can become parents through the process of adoption—by accepting a child with love and grace into their home. Adoption brings with it all the nurturing and blessings of a family upon the child.

What if a church with no youth or children were to take on this model of adoption? I don't know what that would look like other than it has potential for a church to experience connecting with children and youth totally out of grace—with no strings attached. There may be a nearby daycare, school, or housing project that a childless congregation could "adopt" and begin serving—inviting those children and youth into relationship without any expectations of them starting a youth program or joining the church (though, of course, this would be welcome).

Churches with no youth can start experiencing the kingdom by being a presence at local school functions, too. A group of adults could make it their mission (with proper security clearance) to volunteer in the lunchroom or at after-school activities. Start a free tutoring service that meets once a week at the church or in a building close to the school. Offer to feed the football team and the marching band before a home game. Adults in any congregation can (and should) pray for youth, tell their stories to youth, work alongside youth, encourage youth, and cheer them on in their efforts. None of these things requires the youth attend your church, but all lead an adult into a better understanding of Christ and a fuller experience of the kingdom of God.

I recently visited a church in Cedartown, Georgia. Kresge Memorial United Methodist Church is a small church in a small community, and the congregation is growing older. In fact, the congregations of all the churches in Cedartown are growing older. I was told there are very few ministries for children and youth to be involved in there.

A few years ago, church leaders at Kresge realized that though their own church had very few children, God was pointing them across town to where there were neighborhoods full of kids with single-parent families, poor living conditions, troubles with the law, and little to no understanding of the

Bible. The leaders at Kresge decided to do something about it.

They started a Wednesday night children's program. Twenty to thirty adults (almost all of them over 60 years of age) borrowed some vans from nearby churches and began to pick up kids, drive them to the church, feed them, give them some Scripture and a lesson, and, most of all, spend time with them as a community of faith. The numbers quickly grew as kids found out there was a place for them (and as parents realized their kids were being helped during this time).

As the numbers grew, the space did not. After a couple years, some of the children became teenagers (which they're prone to do). Eventually those who were middle and high school age needed a different kind of program. More vans were needed and more space was necessary if everyone was going to be able to meet and carry out the ministry. Kresge contacted other churches in the area. Some churches from nearby towns offered vans and drivers, and two churches in nearby cities started a program similar to Kresge's to reach the same kids—offering the children three choices on Wednesday evenings.

The thing that's hard to believe, though, is that some churches turned down this opportunity. Not only did they refuse to start a program of their own (one that was necessary if the older high school youth were to continue in ministry), but these churches wouldn't even lend their van on Wednesday evenings. Their response communicated, "We don't want them here."

We don't want them here.

What does it take for a church to voice those words? (Perhaps the question is, what has to be lacking in a church for them to be able to voice those words?)

I can't help but listen for Christ's response to those who tell children, "We don't want you here." If our young demonstrate what it means to be in the kingdom and we don't want them, then how will we experience God's kingdom? If we turn away the young from our midst—whether we're shutting them out of our church as in Cedartown, or keeping them in a youth room or building as in the silos of so many churches—then will Christ respond, "Truly I tell you, whatever you did not do for one of the least of these, you did not do for me" (Matthew 25:45)?

Before we become too judgmental toward those other churches in Cedartown, we should look within our own congregations. What are we telling our youth when we push them outside to a youth house across the parking lot, or when we set up their own worship service in another part of the building where they cannot be seen or heard? When we leave teenagers in their separate spaces at the party without inviting them to join us at the food table, are we not also implying, "We don't want you here"? Even if that is not our intention, it may be what they learn. The impact and blessing of a celebration and a community is in its integration and its diversity—where adults and youth can encounter each one's experiences of God's grace and love in their lives.

The full feast of food and fellowship—the stuff that enriches our faith and helps us participate deeply in the celebration of the gospel—comes to us through interaction with the diverse group of people that make up the church. That diversity is a blessing, opening our eyes and hearts to the many ways God is alive and active in each ministry and each individual.

You can help your church reclaim its blessing of diverse communion by passing on these ideas to church leaders. Help them recognize the calling to be one body made up of many parts that interact—each part working in coordination with the rest of the parts to transform the world.

# ENDNOTES

1.  Mark Oestreicher, *Youth Ministry 3.0: A Manifesto of Where We've Been, Where We Are, and Where We Need to Go* (Grand Rapids, MI: Zondervan/Youth Specialties, 2008).

2.  This is far too short a synopsis of pages 73–75 of Marko's manifesto. While there are a few other references to *Youth Ministry 3.0* in this book, I encourage you to pick up your own copy and let it stir your mind and heart. Marko explains the progression of youth ministry over time through three basic adolescent tasks of identity, autonomy, and affinity.

3.  I am not in any way suggesting that we rework Paul's words—I am using his idea to point out how we in the church body today might be divided in a way that doesn't allow us to work together as a community.

4.  Charles R. Foster, *From Generation to Generation: The Adaptive Challenge of Mainline Protestant Education in Forming Faith*, (Eugene, Oregon: Wipf & Stock Publishers, 2012), 41.

5.  Foster, 42.

6.  Oestreicher, 49.

7.  Andrew Root and Kenda Creasy Dean, *The Theological Turn in Youth Ministry* (Downers Grove, IL: IVP Books, 2011), 28.

8.  Foster, 43.

9.  Patricia Hersch, *A Tribe Apart: A Journey into the Heart of American Adolescence* (New York: Fawcett Columbine, 1998),

10. Oestreicher, 58.

11. Mark DeVries, *Sustainable Youth Ministry*, (Downers Grove, IL: IVP Books, 2008), 11.

12. "Willow Creek Repents?" *Parse*, October 18, 2007, www.

christianitytoday.com/parse/2007/october/willow-creek-repents.html.

13. Scott McDonnell, "LifeWay Research Finds Reasons 18- to 22-year-olds Drop Out of Church," LifeWay.com, August 7, 2007, www.lifeway.com/Article/LifeWay-Research-finds-reasons-18-to-22-year-olds-drop-out-of-church.

14. Ed Stetzer, "Leadership Book Interview: Kara Powell," *The Exchange* blog, posted October 18, 2011, www.christianitytoday.com/edstetzer/2011/october/leadership-book-interview-kara-powell.html.

15. DeVries, 11.

16. Kara Powell and Brad Griffin, "The Church Sticking Together: The Vital Role of Intergenerational Relationships in Fostering Sticky Faith," http://stickyfaith.org/articles/the-church-sticking-together.

17. Powell and Griffin, "The Church Sticking Together."

18. Foster, 28.

19. Foster, 32.

20. Drury spoke at The Youth Cartel's The Summit in November 2012. Go to https://www.youtube.com/watch?v=Y4x2o9OK-IN8&feature=youtu.be and watch Dr. Drury's 17-minute talk about congregations where teenagers have a voice. I love what she says in this video: When someone has a hard time talking about something, that person often has a hard time believing that thing is true. If we can't talk about our faith, we will have a hard time taking our faith seriously. When we talk about our faith, we become more faithful people.

21. Specifically, what Marko says is, "For teenage faith formation, verbalization of belief is more important than the accuracy of the beliefs." Check out other great youth ministry insights in his November 11, 2013 blog post entitled "Teenage Faith Formation Grenade," http://whyismarko.com/

teenage-faith-formation-grenade/.

22. For a more complete explanation of Wesley's three ways that we experience grace, go to http://gbgm-umc.org/umw/wesley/walk.stm.

23. Kara Powell, foreword to *Join Generations: Becoming Unashamedly Intergenerational,* by Matthew Deprez (AtlantiCreative, 2013).

24. April L. Diaz, *Redefining the Role of the Youth Worker: A Manifesto of Integration* (La Mesa, California: The Youth Cartel, 2013), 51.

25. Mark Riddle, *Inside the Mind of Youth Pastors: A Church Leader's Guide to Staffing and Leading Youth Pastors* (Grand Rapids, MI: Zondervan/Youth Specialties, 2008), 21.

26. Delia Halverson (Mom and Grandma to our family) has been a Christian educator for over 35 years. She's led countless workshops and written more books than I can count (although I'm sure Amazon can tell you—http://www.amazon.com/Delia-Halverson/e/B00DWE0M7M).

27. Andrew Root, back cover of *Revisiting Relational Youth Ministry* (Downers Grove, IL: IVP Books, 2007).

28. Elizabeth Corrie, *Transforming the Conflict of Youth and Adults: Youth Ministry and Peacebuilding* (publisher, forthcoming).

29. Root, 15.

30. The five adults to one teenager ratio is supported and taught by those promoting the Sticky Faith ideas (http://stickyfaith.org/articles/the-church-sticking-together). Chap Clark is a professor at Fuller Seminary where Sticky Faith originates. His book, *Hurt: Inside the World of Today's Teenagers* (Baker Academic, 2004), has become a textbook and resource for many who are interested in understanding the world and experiences of teenagers. You can read an interesting Q&A with Dr. Clark about his book at http://

fulleryouthinstitute.org/articles/hurt.

31. Riddle, 21.

32. *United Methodist Hymnal* (The United Methodist Publishing House), 48-49.

33. At a recent annual conference of all the UM churches in North Georgia, we wanted to address youth, children's, young adult, campus, and camping ministries. At first the planning team was coming up with ways to help churches boost their programming, but at one point someone on the team said, "Aren't we doing this in such a way that we're just building up the silos? And what about churches who have no youth or children? How do we get them to even listen to what we have to say?" We realized we needed to bring the ministry ideas into line with basic ministries that exist in every church, and then show how to incorporate those age groups into these four basic church ministries of worship, hospitality, service, and discipleship.

34. The website of Erwin McManus, promotional material for his book, *The Artisan Soul*, www.erwinmcmanus.com/.

35. Delia Halverson, *The Gift of Hospitality: In Church, In the Home, In All of Life* (Atlanta: Chalice Press, 1999), 11.

36. www.thementoringproject.org/.

37. Diaz, 105.

38. Diaz, 106.

39. Oestreicher, 53.

40. Foster, 10.

41. *Miz Lil and the Chronicles of Grace* is republished through Zondervan (2004) and is available on Kindle too. Wangerin is an insightful storyteller who connects what God is doing in the world throughout all of his stories.

42. Foster, 26.